BAD NEWS FOR MCENROE

BAD NEWS FOR McENROE

BLOOD, SWEAT, AND BACKHANDS
WITH JOHN, JIMMY, ILIE, IVAN,
BJORN, AND VITAS

BILL SCANLON
WITH
SONNY LONG AND CATHY LONG

ST. MARTIN'S PRESS ≋

NEW YORK

Library of Congress-in-Publication Data
Scanlon, Bill.
   Bad news for McEnroe : blood, sweat, and backhands with John, Jimmy, Ilie, Ivan,
Bjorn, and Vitas / Bill Scanlon with Sonny and Cathy Long.—1st ed.
      p. cm.
   ISBN 0-312-33280-7
   EAN 978-0312-33280-8
   1. Tennis—History.   2. Tennis players.   3. McEnroe, John, 1959–   I. Long, Sonny.
II. Long, Cathy.   III. Title.
GV992.S33 2004
797.342'09—dc22

                                                                    2004050712

First Edition: September 2004

10 9 8 7 6 5 4 3 2 1

CONTENTS

BAD NEWS FOR MCENROE

PROLOGUE

JOHN MCENROE PREPARED to serve. You know, the overex-aggerated preparation we've all seen so many times, back turned to the court and arms hanging straight down to gently touch the head of his racket to the court before going into his windup. He leaned forward and rocked slowly. And then he stopped.

I stood at the other end of the court. It was the quarterfinals of the TransAmerica event at the Cow Palace in San Francisco. After splitting the first two sets, I'd gotten an early break in the third and now McEnroe prepared to serve at 15-all.

It was September 1981. Earlier that year, John had defeated Bjorn Borg to win the Wimbledon title, ending Borg's five-year winning streak in the world's premier event. He followed by defeating Borg to take the U.S. Open title. He was now the undisputed number-one player in the world—and he knew it. The two events that I had won in 1981 (the New Zealand Open and the WCT Championships in Salisbury) were less spectacular but helped raise my confidence—and my ranking back into the top thirty.

My previous win over John in the semifinals of Maui in 1978

gave me a measure of confidence that I could play with this guy. On two other occasions, I held match points before finally losing. For some reason I always played well against John. Every encounter was hard-fought and filled with all the distractions that would become McEnroe legend.

My best friend, Richard Peyton, sat in the front row of the stands. He had been there for my win in Maui, helping me to cope with McEnroe's stall-and-delay tactics. Mostly the antics followed the same old routine: arguments with the umpire, insults aimed at linespeople, and the occasional temper tantrum. Richard and I had talked at length about taking them in stride.

Once more John leaned over and began the rocking motion that would prepare him to serve. And again he stood up. After a couple of beats for dramatic effect, he started walking toward the net and he was talking—to me. I looked over to Richard to gauge his reaction, and he just shrugged his shoulders. This was new and we didn't know what to make of it.

John continued toward the net—I couldn't hear him over the crowd noise, so I approached the net as well. The Cow Palace was packed, but as I reached the net the room got real quiet real fast. Given our history, I'm sure everyone was wondering what would happen next. What did happen next still blows my mind.

Most of our matches degenerated into John screaming something or other across the net, but this time John stood no more than five feet away from me, separated only by the net, and proceeded to logically, rationally, and lucidly explain to me why I shouldn't be beating him. Seriously.

No tantrum, no outburst, just phrases like "Don't you know who I am?"; . . . "not in the same league with me . . ."; "You don't deserve to be on the same court as me . . ."; and "Do you think these people in the crowd really want to watch you play tomorrow instead of me?"

I listened patiently, absolutely amazed. I literally wondered if he knew what he was doing—could he have totally lost it? Could he actually believe that I should throw the match just because he was the higher-ranked star? The umpire started penalizing McEnroe for delays—first a point, then another, then a game. Over McEnroe's shoulder I noticed Barry MacKay, the tournament promoter, pacing frantically in the wings. He was talking and gesturing to the tournament referee. No doubt he was petrified that the umpire would default McEnroe, leaving the crowd to see me tomorrow after all. There's a possibility that Barry had paid McEnroe an appearance guarantee to play in the event, and if so, that investment was looking shaky.

Then, as abruptly as it started, John stopped talking, turned around, and walked to the baseline. Again I was dumbfounded— left standing alone there in the center of the court, wondering if what I had just experienced was real.

As I returned to the baseline, I spoke to the umpire and insisted he reverse all the penalties—we'd play from the original score. I don't know if I'm the only player in the game ever to offer John a scoring advantage, but it just seemed to be the right thing to do. When the umpire announced the reversals, the crowd went nuts. McEnroe just shook his head.

Play continued, and I managed to go on to win. McEnroe and I shook hands at the net and I wondered what he might say. He never met my eye and he never said a word.

The crowd filled the stands to watch me lose in the semifinals the next day, though I'm sure John was right—they'd rather have been watching him. His number-one ranking was secure as both player and box-office attraction. But in a strange way the episode illuminates the drama that was playing out on several levels in the tennis world during what I feel is the greatest era ever in the history of the sport.

While I was caught up in the competition of our match that day in San Francisco, for John the bigger picture was his stature at the top of the rankings. Barry MacKay, along with every other promoter in the sport, was dependent on the star system to sell sponsorships and fill the stands, while political bodies and national associations battled for power in the governance of the sport. Big Money had commercialized the sport and sports agents, a relatively new phenomenon, fueling price wars for appearance fees and endorsement sponsorships while at the same time representing the events and manufacturers who signed the checks.

It was the first generation of professional tennis and the sport was being revolutionized on every level. From players' unions to technological advances in equipment, no area was left untouched and it all played out in front of an international audience, thanks to huge media attention and a popular culture that embraced McEnroe, Connors, Borg, Vilas, Lendl, and Becker as celebrities who transcended the sport.

1:

STAR QUALITY

FLUSHING MEADOWS, NEW YORK, August 1988. The U.S. Open. The Super Bowl of tennis and the toughest Grand Slam tournament in the world. Outside the stadium, in Parking Lot A, there was a revolution. The Association of Tennis Professionals (ATP) players' union, under the leadership of former White House Chief of Staff Hamilton Jordan, was about to turn the tennis world upside down. Frustrated by years of pent-up frustrations, they gathered to announce their withdrawal from tennis's governing body, the Men's International Professional Tennis Council (MIPTC), and the formation of their own proprietary series of events, the ATP Tour.

Inside the grounds, on Stadium Court, another revolution? Not really. Just Andre Agassi kicking Jimmy Connors's ass. Another brash, confident young rebel coming of age. Andre Agassi wasn't the first. We'd seen this play out several times before, young gate-crashers named Becker, Edberg, Lendl, McEnroe, Connors, and Borg, each of whom seemed determined to outdo the last at making a dramatic entrance.

Agassi wasn't even mildly intimidated. The feisty eighteen-

5

year-old had already incurred Connors's wrath by having the nerve to take the first two sets and lead handily in the third. Undaunted, he played as if it was his preordained right to claim his position at the top of the tennis world. Naturally Connors was none too pleased. But the kid went a step further: He managed to infuriate John McEnroe during the match as well.

It was a sight to behold. Standing at the service line as bold as you please, Agassi went into an exquisite parody of McEnroe's trademark sidewinder serve, twisting and gyrating like some angst-ridden soul. He then had the audacity to turn right smack-dab to Johnny Mac, who was seated in a courtside box with his first wife, Tatum O'Neal, and *wink*. Tatum almost fell out of the box, she was laughing so hard. John just glared.

Tickets to the U.S. Open: $200.00; souvenir program: $15.00; hot dog: $8.00 (seriously); an ice-cold Coca-Cola: $3.50; seeing John McEnroe turn purple—*priceless*!

Andre Agassi had arrived, and he would lead the charge into the next generation not just with reams of talent but with that indefinable something that would make him a star. He seemed the perfect, natural extension of tennis's path at that time: lots of talent and a brash demeanor suited perfectly for Arthur Ashe Stadium.

But he turned out to be the last. A sport that was brimming with stars named Becker, Gerulaitis, Borg, Connors, Vilas, Nastase, Panatta, and McEnroe in the '70s and '80s suddenly seemed to be left with one in the '90s: Andre Agassi.

I don't mean for one minute to discredit Pete Sampras or Michael Chang or Jim Courier. They were great talents who wrote plenty of new chapters for the history books. Sampras won more Grand Slam singles titles than any other male tennis player in the history of the sport. They gave us some great entertainment and exciting matches, and I am a player who actually appreciates the purity of their ambitions. No hidden agendas, just great tennis for the sake of great tennis.

All have now retired, barely reaching the age of thirty before calling it quits. Each is a millionaire many times over and looking forward to new challenges in their lives. They were all great champions and likable guys. I even sponsored Sampras for membership at my club, Bel Air Country Club in Los Angeles. But make no mistake, at the end of the day, the paying public wants showmanship and entertainment. And Agassi was the only star.

First rule in the entertainment world: Stars Sell.

First rule of tennis: Stars Sell.

In the previous generation of tennis players, it was enough to be an exceptional player. Priorities were different then and the audience valued sportsmanship over showmanship. It was even considered to be bad taste to draw attention to yourself. Players such as Laver, Rosewall, Emerson, Smith, Ashe, Newcombe, and Roche were leaders by example and coaches like Harry Hopman would tolerate no cutups.

That's probably the main reason that I took up the game as a kid. My parents were so impressed by those very champions that they encouraged (pushed) me hard into the sport.

By the commercialized '70s, a lot had changed. In the world and in our sport. Now the emphasis was on making the most of your talent in the market. Thanks to superagents like Mark McCormack and Donald Dell, there was a lot at stake beyond just winning tennis matches. It wasn't enough now just to win—now a player needed to entertain. He had to have charisma. He had to have star quality and if he did, well, that could translate into major ad campaigns and big bucks.

Tennis was entertainment. Tournaments were selling stars.

How had tennis gone from the personification of the gentleman player/sportsman, such as Rod Laver, a quiet, unassuming nice guy with his clean-cut haircut and baggy shorts, to "molding" players into sellable images?

Part of the answer, I'm sure, lies in the fact that our generation was a product of its time. Television had emerged in the '60s as a medium of maximum exposure and we were fascinated with rock 'n' roll and the lifestyle images it evoked. Larger-than-ife personalities like Muhammad Ali, the Beatles, and the Rolling Stones were thrust into our living rooms and into our consciousnesses. It opened the door for a whole new set of rules.

IN THE TENNIS WORLD the first larger-than-life personality to emerge was Ilie Nastase. Without actually giving any thought to creating an image, Nastase was just naturally a character. Criticize him as disgraceful, criticize him as unsportsmanlike, criticize him as obscene, but buy a ticket because he was a box-office bonanza—a star who could fill a stadium. From the moment he set foot on the court it was anybody's guess what would happen or how the match might end up. He could evoke laughter, tears, anger, frustration, sympathy, or hatred—all in the same match, depending whose side you were on.

A veritable genius with a tennis racquet and the first player to be ranked number one on the ATP computer, Nastase was sheer poetry in motion. It's hard to name a player who was more naturally gifted. His brilliance and artistry and speed afoot carried him to the U.S. Open title in 1972, the French Open title in 1973, four Masters Championships, two Italian Open titles, and another fifty-one miscellaneous tournament wins.

The pages of this chapter could be filled by recounting Nastase's exploits alone. His on-court persona drove his opponents insane, but fans loved him. How could they help it? Certainly he berated linespersons, but he was also known to kiss them, mid-match, in front of God and country—usually the pretty female ones—but, hey, if a very bearded decidedly male linesperson gave him the benefit of a close call, Ilie just might give him a big, fat wet one and drop to his knees and kiss the line as well.

Nastase was the first player I ever played against in a professional tournament. It was the first round of the Arkansas Classic in Little Rock and I was still a sophomore at Trinity University. Naturally I was in awe and probably as much entertained by my opponent as anyone in the crowd that night. I won a set and thought it was the best day of my tennis life.

At the staid and proper Wimbledon in 1975, the most unstaid and utterly improper Ilie Nastase delighted the gallery when he disagreed with the chair's decision not to call a rain delay. Ilie's tactic? He went into the stands and retrieved an umbrella from one of the fans, then proceeded to receive serve from Dick Stockton, racket in his right hand and umbrella in his left.

Wimbledon's response may well have been: "We are not amused," but the crowd was certainly amused. Entertained like never before and loving every minute of it. Nastase lost the match to Stockton that day, but he posted yet another PR victory.

In 1977 at Wimbledon, Ilie actually *hid* from an umpire who presumed to act as Ilie's disciplinarian that day. During a dispute over yet another line call on Court Two, Ilie sought cover behind the fence—in the bushes. The umpire didn't care for it at all, and neither did Nastase's opponent Andrew Pattison, but the fans— well, you know. No doubt for many years there were casual tennis players in London who recalled having been there "on the day when Nastase . . ."

To comply with (or as protest of) an apparel rule that stipulated that doubles teams must wear matching attire, Nastase, while playing doubles with Arthur Ashe, deemed it necessary to paint his face black. While I'm sure some politically correct automatons found this to be in poor taste, with Nastase you can only laugh because the joke was on the absurdity of the all-white-apparel rule (that still exists at Wimbledon)—not on the fact that Ashe was an African American. Ashe personally cracked up laughing.

Before Wimbledon in 1978, Nastase had a dream. He won the coveted championship and ran round Centre Court with the trophy proudly raised in his left hand; of course his middle finger was proudly raised in his right. Ilie Nastase, an innately gifted player who was defiant to the core.

Fans recognized that there were these two very distinct sides to

Ilie. At the 1981 French Open, fans voted him two awards: one was for his good humor and the other for being the worst sport. He had sinned and was granted absolution.

Nastase's antics almost always entertained his spectators, though there were occasional exceptions. In the finals in Dubai while playing Wojtek Fibak, Ilie Nastase went through a few of his patented X-rated gestures and various other pieces of his repertoire. Seated in his royal box, Shaikh Hamdan was most assuredly not amused. Ilie was forced to write a letter of apology, which then appeared in English and Arabic in newspapers throughout the Gulf region.

With the exception of myself, Ilie rarely amused his opponents. Players called him "Nasty," but to Romanians he was simply their *baiat rau*, "the naughty boy," petulant and pouty like the little boy who takes his ball and goes home when things don't go his way. He could curse, charm, and cajole; he could infuriate, intimidate, and endear.

No doubt about it, tennis had become entertainment: stars with huge drawing power playing before huge crowds in televised events. By 1972 the WCT (World Championship Tennis) Finals in Dallas between Rod Laver and Ken Rosewall had demonstrated that tennis was good for television. Huge ratings meant that tennis had become *showbiz*.

IN THE TENNIS WORLD there may have been no better showman, regardless of talent or rankings, than Vitas Gerulaitis. Gerulaitis was sheer electricity on-court and it was mesmerizing to see him race from one corner of the court to the other, his blond hair flying behind him. But mostly Vitas was known for his playboy image.

Vitas landed on the tour in the mid-'70s, just as the disco craze was taking over the world. *Saturday Night Fever* was the summer's hottest movie and the Bee Gees were on top of the charts. Another legendary icon of the time opened right in Vitas's backyard—

Studio 54. It was the nightclub of the stars and Vitas was a regular, hanging out with *Sports Illustrated* swimsuit model Cheryl Tiegs and other starlets. He also managed to "drag" a few of his tennis cronies along most of the time, players such as Nastase, Bjorn Borg, and Adrianno Panatta.

Few players actively cultivated an image as much as Vitas. He was one of the first tour players to realize that building a reputation away from the court could reap big rewards. It worked. Vitas was very highly ranked and was always competitive in the majors, but apart from winning the 1977 Australian Open, he never managed a major Grand Slam title.

You wouldn't know it from his bankbook.

Gerulaitis was marketed as a sex symbol and he commanded endorsement contracts and appearance fees well beyond what would have been normal for a player with his achievements. He also collected mansions and Rolls-Royces—several of each. The girls just loved him, and he loved the girls. Vintage Vitas: At the U.S. Open in 1981 after his stunning upset victory over Ivan Lendl in the fourth round, Vitas Gerulaitis blew kisses to the crowd. Twenty years later, that's a common gesture: blowing kisses to all four corners of the stadium. Back then it was something only Vitas could pull off.

When I first turned pro as the NCAA (National Collegiate Athletic Association) champion in 1976, I was recruited by the big management firms IMG (International Management Group) and ProServ (Professional Services, Inc.) I was also approached by Bill Riordan, a sometimes tournament promoter who had formerly managed Jimmy Connors. I have to say that I was very impressed with the presentations that were offered by each of these agents. We had several meetings and I gave it a lot of thought. After much consideration, I signed with IMG and Bob Kain.

I'm sure that part of my decision was based on the fact that Bob also represented Vitas Gerulaitis and Bjorn Borg. Bob and his colleague Bud Stanner told me they were going to "mold" me as a marketable image. Those were their exact words: *mold me.* Like I was some piece of Play-Doh. It sounded okay to me. Anything that worked for Gerulaitis and Borg would be just fine. Where do I sign?

You know the phrase "Image is everything." Agents scrambled not just to represent their clients, but to "create" them. Gerulaitis became the jet-setter playboy, Borg the teen angel, Panatta the Roman god, and Vilas the soulful poet. Their trendsetting ways made long hair, headbands, and tight shorts the vogue among players and made the girls swoon. That's what tennis was all about. Of course, as a young, somewhat naïve kid from Texas, it was also a bit distracting.

When I joined the tour the top-ranked players in the world were Borg, Connors, Nastase, Vilas, and Gerulaitis. Who wouldn't look up to them as role models? The problem is that they were also the top-ranked playboys in the world. Every week, every night, every town—remember, this was the '70s. You could forgive a kid for thinking that this was a pretty good life.

Vitas and I won the doubles title in Adelaide, Australia, one year and couldn't fly to Perth for the next tournament until Monday afternoon. When we arrived there was only one suite left at the tournament hotel, so we shared. It was a front-row seat to one of the wildest shows I'd ever seen. Most nights we stayed up late—there was a lot to learn about Perth after midnight. Friday night we didn't sleep at all. I had lost in the quarterfinals, but Vitas was due to play his semifinals on Saturday. I sat and listened as Vitas called the tournament director at about 9:00 A.M. to explain that he was sick and would have to default.

The tournament director would have none of it. He pleaded with Gerulaitis to at least show up for the match, even if he had to quit halfway through. Vitas showed, and he won. Then he won the finals. Nice example for an aspiring tennis pro.

———

BJORN BORG MANAGED ONE of the more remarkable feats of image building. He did it very quietly. That is to say, he kept his thoughts to himself.

As the tennis world was just getting used to the shock (and volume) of Nastase and Jimmy Connors, Borg arrived with long blond hair, a headband, skintight Fila shirts, and he never said a word. Ever. Good calls, bad calls, winning, losing—it didn't matter to Bjorn—he just played and offered an expression that seemed to indicate he knew something you didn't. And the teenaged girls in London went gaga over him.

One of the perks that is extended to Wimbledon tennis players is the famous courtesy cars that will chauffeur them to and from the All England Lawn Tennis & Croquet Club at their whim. Borg eschewed the perk. He preferred to stay in the far north of London where he had a special arrangement with the Holiday Inn Swiss Cottage and the nearby Cumberland Tennis Club. He also had an endorsement contract with Swedish automobile maker Saab, which provided a car for Bjorn's use during Wimbledon. His driver? Coach Lennart Bergelin, of course, but only so far as the West Gate Parking Lot.

The teenaged girls were so Borg-crazy that it was impossible for him even to make the two-hundred-yard walk from the parking lot to the locker room inside the grounds. And so Borg transferred to a Wimbledon courtesy car every day for the last leg of the journey.

Prior to 1980, there were precious few grass tennis courts available to Wimbledon players in London. This may come as a shock, but the All England Club had for years leased the land adjoining the championships (now known as Aorangi Park and used to provide twelve practice-only courts for the players) to the New Zealand Club and those courts were off-limits to players in the tournament. Because of this phenomenon, part of the challenge of winning at Wimbledon was negotiating to get sufficient practice time on the grass. Players went to great lengths to get it done.

Borg actually chose a hotel more than an hour away from the tournament site so that he would have unlimited practice time at the Cumberland Club.

The "teen angel" who first appeared at Wimbledon in its strike year gradually morphed into the "cool Swede." Baby-blue eyes that had driven schoolgirls into a frenzy at Wimbledon in 1973 were ice blue now, sending players into a frenzy. That was his act.

It really was an act; not one designed to emotionally grip an audience, but one with the specific purpose of strangle-holding his opponent in a psychological grip. Inside he seethed. Or so we were told time and time again in the interviews that he granted. He claimed to have had a terrible temper, so bad that it cost him matches in his youth and now his only hope was to stifle it completely. The solution was to never allow even the slightest hint of reaction or even acknowledgment of success or failure on the court.

We were told that Borg's coach, Lennart Bergelin, was on the receiving end of many an off-court explosion following some disappointing match, but on court Borg maintained that icy façade. It was one impressive schtick. Seriously, in an era of players clammering over one another to be the most vocal, Borg spoke the loudest without ever making a sound.

Borg's best friend on the tour was Vitas Gerulaitis. They spent a lot of time together on and off the court. Nobody could mistake the two personalities—as opposite as fire and ice. But with their matching long blond hair, there were times when Vitas Gerulaitis was mistaken for Bjorn Borg. Not usually, though, when they were together. Once, in an elevator, a fan made that very mistake and asked Vitas for his (Borg's) autograph. He was standing next to Borg at the time! In typical Gerulaitis fashion, Vitas obligingly signed—Borg's name.

NO AMOUNT OF IDOLATRY could surpass the adulation bestowed by the devoted legions upon their Roman god, Adrianno Panatta, and their mantra chorus of *"Aaaa—dri—aaaano!"* At the Foro Italico, columns still rise to surround the center court and thou shalt have no other gods before Adrianno Panatta. The fans in the seats abided by the commandment; the people calling the lines abided by it as well. Woe be to any player on the opposite side of the net on Campo Centrale.

Tennis players are known to expect silence from the crowd while they play. It's a long-standing tradition that goes along with the absence of movement in the stands during points. These players found a surprise waiting for them at Foro. Any match involving an Italian was more likely to resemble a clash among gladiators at the Coliseum. If that Italian happened to be Panatta . . .

It was sheer bloodlust that sent most players straight to default. Harold Solomon refused to play on after a series of bad calls blatant in their favoritism. José Higueras stormed off in disgust, abruptly bringing his match to an end after being pelted by coins that were tossed from the stands.

I played Panatta on Campo Centrale at the Italian Open in Rome. I lost. It seemed the prudent thing to do.

BJORN BORG WASN'T MOST PLAYERS. In the final of the 1978 Italian Open, Borg calmly endured the chanting, bad calls, hurled obscenities, and even the coins. He was absolutely unflappable and simply claimed the title.

JIMMY CONNORS WAS A STAR everywhere he went, but center stage for Jimmy was the U.S. Open. New Yorkers loved him, and he loved them. As a brash kid fresh from St. Louis, Connors began his summer in 1974 by trouncing Ken Rosewall in the finals of Wimbledon. Arriving in New York City eight weeks later, Connors pronounced, "At the U.S. Open there will be a hundred and twenty-seven losers and me!"

He was right and they loved it. Trounced Rosewall again in the final. Everywhere he went at Forest Hills he was flanked by two very large, very intimidating bodyguards. And he wore tassels on his socks like Muhammad Ali.

In 1975 the USTA convinced the West Side Tennis Club to switch its court surface from grass to clay. Seriously. It has never been proven exactly which brain surgeon at the USTA actually suggested that Americans should prefer to play their national championships on their least favorite surface, but it really did happen.

Connors lost in the finals to Manuel Orantes, a Spanish clay court specialist. And the crowd loved him more. In 1976, still on clay, Jimbo beat Borg in the finals in front of a full house with girlfriend Marjorie Wallace (Miss Universe) in the players' box with his mom, Gloria. The crowd? You know it.

In 1978 when the U.S. Open found a new home in Flushing Meadows, the early years could only be described as "the U.S. Public Parks Championships." The West Side Tennis Club in Forest Hills had been refined. Ivy covered the walls and red brick sidewalks led past traditional homes in an upscale neighborhood. Beautiful grass courts spread out before the clubhouse and its familiar terraces. The club had decades of tradition and ghosts of Tilden and Budge floating through the halls. Even with clay courts the place reeked of class.

The brand-new USTA Tennis Center was nothing but concrete, steel, and chain-link fences. The only thing that reeked was the locker rooms. Built on the World's Fair grounds next door to Shea Stadium, airplanes competed with trains to see which could be more distracting. It was only fitting that the inaugural champion should be the best street fighter in the game, Jimmy Connors. He played like he owned the place.

SOME PLAYERS CAPTIVATED VIEWERS like the Hollywood matinee idols of the silver screen. Guillermo Vilas, brown hair streaming to his shoulders and brown eyes reflecting his poet's soul, was a matinee idol. Labor Day, U.S. Open 1977: On the Stadium Court at Forest Hills, tournament referee Mike Blanchard tried to move the Vilas match with José Higueras from the afternoon matinee to the evening performance. Blanchard was a veteran of many U.S. Opens—he should have known better. A crowd of more than twelve thousand shouted, "We won't go!" And they didn't. Blanchard wisely reconsidered.

When Vilas went on to win the U.S. Open title that year over Jimmy Connors, the crowd lifted him and swept him from the stadium amid resounding cheers of *"Vee-las."*

Of course Vilas gave his fans plenty of ammunition to support his image. He did publish a book of self-authored poems. The volume was entitled *Ciento Veinte Cinco (One Hundred Twenty-Five)* and no explanation was ever given as to the significance of the number. His musical talents, though modest at the time, were also offered on a record album (back before CDs) and his Argentinean fans made it a bestseller.

Vilas's celebrity was enhanced by the constant presence of his chain-smoking coach/manager/mentor/Svengali Ion Tiriac. The dark Transylvanian had mentored Nastase before turning his full attention to Vilas in the mid-'70s, but it was the student who followed Vilas that redefined celebrity. His name was Boris Becker.

AS BUSINESS PARTNERS ON and off the court, Vilas and Tiriac invested in young Boris Becker in the early '80s, paying his parents a guarantee and promising to guide the kid to the top of the tennis world. It was a short trip.

Becker won Wimbledon at the age of seventeen. And again at the age of eighteen. He was such a burst of positive energy that it was impossible not to root for him. There were no outbursts to remind us of McEnroe or Connors. He wasn't quiet and mysterious like Borg or Vilas. He just played tennis as if he truly loved every minute of it, and the world loved watching him. He would emerge from matches bloodied and scraped—by the court—for he would dive to the surface to make winning volleys. He was nicknamed "Boom Boom" for his powerful serve—but he asked everyone to stop calling him that because his mother didn't like it. We obliged.

And he opened the floodgates of outside endorsement opportunities. Players had been paid well to endorse products and use branded equipment, but Becker took it to a whole new level. His image allowed the advertising executives on Madison Avenue to view tennis stars as real icons, worthy of full-on advertising campaigns for Mercedes-Benz and Coca-Cola. Becker generously paved the way for his understudy, Andre Agassi.

AGASSI'S CAMPAIGN for Canon cameras said it all: "Image is everything." Of course Andre knew that it helped just a little if you also happened to be one of the best players in the world. He also has shown a lot of substance behind that image over the years on and off the court. Besides becoming one of only five players in history to win all four Grand Slam titles, Agassi has put his stamp on his hometown of Las Vegas, where he operates the Agassi Foundation and the Agassi Academy. These are not tennis camps, but real schools where underachieving kids are recruited and then taught that they can succeed. The results have been astounding. Innovative methods that Andre helped to develop are put into practice and Andre uses his celebrity as a platform to impact the community in a way that will pay dividends for years. Last year the Agassi Foundation held its annual gala to raise funds for the schools. The event featured a number of film, TV, and sports celebrities and earned over $12 million in one night.

While he made short work of Jimmy Connors that day on Stadium Court in the U.S. Open, Agassi actually paid quite a compliment to John McEnroe with his little parody, though John probably never saw it that way.

OF OUR WHOLE GENERATION, John McEnroe was the one player whose act drew audiences like no other. Whether they loved him or hated him, people came to see him. Again and again.

At Wimbledon in 1977, the prodigy just out of high school stunned everyone by going through the qualifying rounds all the way to the semifinals of the championship. The native New Yorker stayed in a small flat in Earl's Court with a couple of other players to share expenses and traveled mostly by the tube (subway). By the time he lost in the semis to Jimmy Connors, he had announced his arrival very loudly. Particularly loudly in the quarterfinals, as it was there that he made his mark as a showman.

McEnroe got upset with himself when he lost the first set to Phil Dent, and he bent his racket under his foot. The spectators in Centre Court, not yet familiar with the John McEnroe who would become such a big part of their culture over the next dozen years, didn't applaud the behavior. Not yet. This year they booed the kid, but he found the booing amusing. He smiled and kicked his racket crosscourt. More booing.

Like any good comic on the most important stage of all, John had found a routine that worked and he liked it. So he milked it for all it was worth. The next day the London tabloids dubbed him "McBrat" and a star was born.

It surprised most of the tennis world that McEnroe decided to retain his amateur status after that great run at Wimbledon. He had in fact committed to attend Stanford and play for at least a year under Dick Gould. He kept that promise, but it didn't keep his star from rising.

After a perfunctory win at the NCAA Championships over John Sadri, John was back making headlines. Of all the characters to adorn the tennis stage, McEnroe was the most . . . colorful. Even Nastase and Connors seemed tame by comparison. John's shows went on to become audience-interactive in ways that could never be scripted. Audiences came to expect histrionics from McEnroe and he was more than willing to oblige.

At Wimbledon 1981, McEnroe, disgusted with himself after

blowing a point or two, turned and screamed the best line I've ever heard on a tennis court: "I'm so disgusting, you shouldn't watch! Everybody leave!"

Everybody stayed.

They loved the performance. One minute he'd be making a beautiful shot and the next an ugly scene. He embodied schizophrenia. He was always condemned, but he was always watched.

Off the court he would manage to draw attention as well. Sometimes it was by the company he kept, usually rock stars like Keith Richards or Eddie Money. As was the case with that other New Yorker, Vitas Gerulaitis, Mac was followed wherever he went. But while Vitas went for champagne and caviar at Studio 54, John was more likely to be found drinking a beer at a recording session or at George Martin's bar on the Upper East Side.

Just to keep us entertained, John married Tatum ("Tantrum") O'Neal. Irish tempers are known to flare and these two held strong to tradition throughout their marriage and long after it was over.

Year after year his one-man show sold tickets; the problem is there was more than one person onstage. Ask anyone who ever played him, and to a man they will tell you it was all an act, a contrived tactic of someone who would do anything to escape losing, an added weapon in the arsenal of a great athlete who would employ any means to gain an edge over his fellow competitors. Usually the tantrums were predictable—occurring just about the time his opponent got onto a hot streak and needed cooling off. It was never a question with McEnroe of *whether* he would argue a call in a match, but how many times, and who would be the target of his wrath.

Biographer Richard Evans said in *A Rage for Perfection,* his bestselling book on John McEnroe, that McEnroe behaved the way he did because he "perceived an injustice had occurred, and injustices must not be tolerated."

To Richard, who I know to be a thoughtful, well-educated, and well-spoken friend, I respond . . .

You CANNOT be serious!

2:

IT'S A DAMN WAR OUT THERE

IN THE FINAL of the U.S. Open in 2002, two aged warriors—a couple of old geezers on the downhill side of thirty going by the names of Pete Sampras and Andre Agassi—faced off against each other for the thirty-fourth time as professionals. The first time these two met on the ATP Tour was in the quarterfinals in Rome's Foro Italico in 1989, but they had been going head to head since Sampras was seven years old and Agassi was eight.

That first time was at a junior tournament in Northridge, California. They would continue to face each other for another seven or eight years as juniors, both in the top of their class and both eschewing all other interests (school, other sports) in a quest for early success on the tour.

From the moment they arrived on the tennis scene, they were heralded as the saviors of American tennis. After John McEnroe's sabbatical, he rarely matched his earlier standards of performance. Connors had aged, pure and simple. He fought gallantly against the clock and gave glimpses of the old fire, but his time had passed. Other Americans, such as Gerulaitis, Gottfried, Stockton, Dibbs, Solomon, and the Mayers (Sandy and Gene), all gradually slipped into retirement and soon we were left hanging on to memories and wondering why there was no new crop of great young Americans.

For the latter half of the '80s, players from all over the rest of the world dominated the game. The United States offered no contenders to fight Becker, Edberg, Lendl, Wilander, Cash, and Mecir. There was a herd of Swedes cornering the market on top twenty rankings and Eastern Europe started pumping out strong players like so many assembly lines. And in the United States? Well, we built great tennis academies headed by Harry Hopman and Nick Bollettieri and they trained the foreigners. Our great college tennis experience? Mostly foreigners—Mikael Pernfors of Sweden won the NCAA's back to back for the University of Georgia.

There is a theory that made the rounds on why America experienced a decline for a few years. It is two-pronged. First, in the '80s a number of new sports, all with big money and plenty of exposure, successfully stole the talented young athletes who might have chosen to pursue tennis. Second, our American tennis "heroes" of the late '70s were not the great role models needed to attract kids and their parents. Hard to imagine the parents of some twelve-year-old hoping that their kid would grow up to be just like Connors or McEnroe.

AND SO SAMPRAS and Agassi arrived in 1989, followed close behind by Michael Chang and Jim Courier. The world, and the United States in particular, couldn't wait. In the beginning it looked as if they would be great champions—and more. What the tennis world wanted—even more than great champions—was rivalries. Connors *vs.* Borg. Borg *vs.* McEnroe. McEnroe *vs.* Lendl. Lendl *vs.* Becker. Heavyweight title bouts.

It looked like the wait was over. Of course these guys would have great matches and early indications were that they were at each other's throats. At one stage Agassi even went so far as to criticize Sampras's boring appearance on the court and remark that he wasn't "fit to be number one in the world."

The media salivated, but Pete's mouth was still agape when Agassi faxed an apology to Sampras. An apology? You could hear the collective moan. Connors would *never* have apologized—especially to McEnroe.

The Sampras–Agassi relationship became, in a word, *nice*. And it stayed nice. To their credit, Agassi and Sampras are both classy guys and they've been that way for the duration of their careers. It's not fake; that's really the way they are. But *classy* never really made for an intense, bitter rivalry. Before that thirty-fourth encounter at the 2002 Open, Sampras fueled the hype in a way that would make any world-class heavyweight tremble: "He brings out the best in me." Fighting words, for sure. Agassi, never to be outdone, responded in kind, saying of Sampras, "Pete's the best I've ever played against."

RIVALRIES DEFINED MY GENERATION—rivalries filled with emotion and rife with comments that left no doubt at all about how one player felt about the other. We dealt with egos so large that no locker room on the tour could hold more than one at a time.

Jimmy Connors was the first of our generation to openly show disdain for his opponents—all of them. His predecessors, Laver, Rosewall, Smith, Ashe, Newcombe, and Roche, were in that same class of well-mannered gentlemen who would never utter a bad word about their fellow competitors. They held to the old traditions of sportsmanship and respect and it showed in their on-court demeanor. If a player got an obviously bad call, his opponent was likely to respond by giving away the next point. It happened even in important matches, as was the case in the WCT Finals in Dallas between Laver and Rosewall. The two were playing for an unprecedented $50,000 first prize and each of them actually donated a point to the other after questionable calls.

Tom Gorman, the popular U.S. Davis Cup player, had a back injury that would occasionally flare up unexpectedly. When it did he knew that he would be unable to play for a couple of days. That was not so unusual. What was unusual was the time he played Stan Smith in the semifinals of an event and tweaked the back. He was winning at the time. Tom could tell that his back would prevent him from playing in the final the next day, so he played his heart out, extended his lead, and reached match point—and then defaulted the match. He felt the tournament and the crowd deserved a final match, so he stepped aside, allowing Smith to advance.

Jimmy Connors flew in the face of every tradition that called for gentlemanly behavior and sportsmanship. To hear him tell the story, he once offered a point to his opponent after a bad call. It was early in his career, and he lost the match. He would never do that again. Quite the opposite, he would fight tooth and nail to get as many bad calls in his favor as possible. In the final of the U.S. Open against Guillermo Vilas, Jimmy was on the good side of a call at a critical point in the match. They were playing on clay at Forest Hills, so there was an obvious ball mark on the court surface, so obvious that it could be clearly seen by television viewers as the camera zoomed closer.

The umpire suggested that the linesman go and inspect the mark to verify his call. Connors got there first and rubbed out the mark with his shoe. End of debate.

In the early years Connors was represented by Bill Riordon, a maverick promoter who enjoyed their roles as outsiders in the prim and proper world of country club tennis. Riordon marketed Jimmy as a street fighter who would have been just as comfortable in the boxing ring as on the tennis court. He modeled his image after the boxers who regularly trash-talked their opponents and boldly announced their intention to "destroy them in the ring."

He also went after them outside the ring. When Connors was banned from the French Open in 1974 for participating in Billie Jean King's World Team Tennis, he filed lawsuits against every-

one in sight and cemented his position way outside the establishment. This was great for tennis as a spectator sport because the
public loved the fight. Frank Chirkanian (legendary CBS Sports
producer) took advantage of the situation and promoted several
"heavyweight title bouts" between Connors and Laver, Newcombe, and so forth, with huge "winner take all" prizes staged at
Caesars Palace in Las Vegas.

Jimmy felt it was his world and anyone who threatened his
position at number one should be brought down in a hurry. He
once said, "People don't seem to understand that it's a damn war
out there." He then set out to declare war on everyone who
crossed his path.

"I'll chase that son of a bitch across the world. Every time he
turns around, he'll see my shadow across him." That classic retort
was a Jimmy Connors special after his crushing defeat in the 1978
Wimbledon final at the hands of Bjorn Borg.

Their rivalry started innocently enough. In October of 1973, a
local Swedish boy, a mere seventeen-year-old, in front of a partisan crowd in Stockholm, scored an upset victory over the game's
resident bully. Fairy-tale stuff.

Connors, being Connors, was undaunted. In 1974 he went on
a tear the likes of which the game hadn't seen since Laver won the
Grand Slam in 1969. Connors won an unbelievable fourteen out
of twenty tournaments, including the Australian Open, Wimbledon, and the U.S. Open. Only his ban from the French Open kept
him from a possible Grand Slam.

Jimmy got his shot at revenge against Borg, "the Boy Wonder," in the U.S. Clay Court Championships and posted his own
win in the finals to add another title to the year's résumé. On his
way to the title at the U.S. Open, he dispatched Borg again in the
semifinals. In fact, after that stunning loss to Borg in Stockholm,
Connors trampled all over Borg in seven straight confrontations
before Borg would beat him again.

And then beat him he did. In five out of six of their next
friendly little meetings, every one of them a final, Borg came out

on top, culminating in that fateful Wimbledon in 1978 and Connors's infamous pronouncement.

Twenty-three times between 1973 and 1981, Borg and Connors battled. Twelve of those were title matches. Eight times they played each other in Grand Slams. Four of those were for titles. Connors won two of their encounters at the U.S. Open; Borg won two at Wimbledon.

Describing his rivalry with Borg, Connors made it very clear how he felt, "We tried to murder each other. That's the only way we know how to play tennis."

Borg added a chipped backhand approach shot to his arsenal in 1978, a backhand that left Connors flabbergasted and flattened. When asked about it, Connors responded, "What backhand?"

It was a prime example of what Borg meant when he said of Connors, "He's the player all other players most want to beat because he can never say his opponent played well."

Borg won five Wimbledons in a row. And six French Opens. Most of those years found Connors at number one on the ATP computer. Connors desperately wanted to define the era—even said so publicly—and he won more tournament titles than any player in history at that time. Pretty good stuff. Unfortunately, it's hard to define an era when some other guy wins the French and Wimbledon every year for five years in a row. The best Jimmy can say is that he outlasted Borg—much in the same way that the Rolling Stones outlasted the Beatles.

BORG'S DEPARTURE from tennis only meant that Jimmy needed to find new enemies. He did. John McEnroe was the first. While Borg was winning the French and Wimbledon, Connors had a small tradition going at the U.S. Open in New York. He managed to win every other year (the even years) in 1974, '76, and '78. Amazingly he won on three different surfaces; grass at Forest Hills in '74, clay (also Forest Hills) in '76, and on hard courts at Flushing Meadows in '78.

McEnroe had the audacity to win the U.S. Open three times in a row, starting in 1979. This was really getting in the way of Connors defining an era. It didn't please Jimmy, either, that McEnroe had usurped his unofficial title of number-one bad sport in the game. Every match between the two was a war. Regardless of the venue, it became important for each to establish a dominance over the other so as to have a mental edge when they met in a major. And the battlegrounds didn't remain inside the court.

Bjorn Borg was universally liked and respected in the tennis world. This made it somewhat difficult for Connors to attack him in the press. There just wasn't a whole lot for Jimmy to criticize about anything Borg did, except that he won too often. Hence Jimmy's "chase the son of a bitch around the world" comment.

McEnroe made life a lot more fun. It was obvious that the two men hated each other: the crown prince and the heir apparent. McEnroe and Connors were so very alike and so very different. Twenty-five years later, they still dislike each other and they still fight over who *was* the bigger star. Now, that's a *rivalry*.

Of course all their matches against each other were in the later rounds with a great deal at stake. They clashed with each other in fourteen title bouts. Connors won seven and McEnroe won seven. They were the final matches that tournament directors salivated over, banked on, for they were in a high-stakes game themselves. Connors–McEnroe matches were entertainment. Before, during, and after the matches, the show never ended.

They refused to stay in the same hotel, and they wouldn't speak to each other in the locker room, but they never passed on an opportunity to speak *at* each other via some media middle man. They perfected the notion that if you can't say something lowdown, dirty, and despicable, then say nothing at all.

By reputation, McEnroe soon supplanted the Connors as Public Enemy Number One. By ranking, his artistry and finesse would surpass Connors for another number-one position. Connors won the clash at Wimbledon in 1977. Connors won the clash at the U.S. Open in 1978. McEnroe won at the U.S. Open in 1979. McEnroe won at the U.S. Open in 1980. That particular clash of the titans went to a fifth-set tiebreaker. In the last two points, Connors netted an easy volley, then sailed a backhand deep. It was an ending he referred to as "the two worst points of my life."

Connors deposed McEnroe for the Wimbledon title in 1982. McEnroe exacted his revenge over Connors there in 1984—Connors was virtually dismantled, 6–1, 6–1, 6–2, a McEnroe display of total domination. McEnroe doubled his pleasure by defeating Connors at the U.S. Open that same year. At the WCT Finals in Dallas against each other, McEnroe held a 2–1 edge. Twice they locked horns at the Masters. Mac won both. To paraphrase Connors—talk about a couple of sons of bitches chasing each other across the world . . .

There were no two rivals so unpredictable or so tempestuous. Trading off the number-one and number-two slots among Americans, and sometimes in the world, the rivalry dominated men's tennis.

For five years Connors could never get past Borg at Wimbledon. Year after year Jimmy tried to stake some sort of claim at the top of the tennis world, always falling just short. When Borg's Wimbledon reign finally did come to an end, it was all the more painful for Connors because it was John McEnroe who pulled the plug.

FOR SIX YEARS Bjorn Borg dominated men's tennis. By the time he was twenty-six years old, he had won eleven major titles, the only blemish on his record being that he never managed to win the U.S. Open. There are no words to adequately express the impact Borg had on the era. Ilie Nastase perhaps best expressed Borg's dominance in tennis: "We should send him to another planet. We play tennis. He plays something else." After losing to the Swede in the 1976 Wimbledon final, Nastase joked, "He's a robot from outer space; a Martian."

He was virtually unbeatable on clay and won forty-one consecutive matches on the grass at Wimbledon, losing only the last he ever played there to John McEnroe. Then Borg, at the age of twenty-six, decided to walk away from the game. He never looked back.

As irritated as Connors was by Borg's winning ways, it was Vitas Gerulaitis who personified frustration at the hands of the Borg machine. After winning their semifinals match in the Masters tournament, his first win following sixteen consecutive losses to Borg, Gerulaitis walked into the press room with an unmistakable scowl on his face. Before any question could be asked, he sat down, pointed his finger at the crowd of reporters, and said, "Nobody beats Vitas Gerulaitis *seventeen* times in a row!" He had a roomful of reporters laughing in the aisles.

In one sense, it's very difficult to even use the word *rivalry* in connection with Borg. No doubt, he was the greatest player of the time. He set such a high standard that the rest of us were forced by his example to raise our level of play. The ultimate sign of success in any player's mind was how well he played against Borg. I know personally one of my most memorable victories was my win over Borg in Tokyo in 1980.

By late October in 1980, Bjorn was the essence of tennis success. He had won fifty-nine out of the sixty-two matches he had played that year, adding titles at Wimbledon, the French Open, and the Masters to his already sizable collection of crowns. The defeat at the hands of a journeyman named Scanlon was the only loss Borg would have before the final of any tournament the entire year. The only explanation I can offer is that Borg simply forced everyone who played him to play the best game they could conceivably muster. He would accept no less from you.

Yes, I can categorize him easily as a rival to many, but my reluctance to use the word *rivalry* in connection with Bjorn Borg stems from the simple observation that I *never* heard him utter a harsh word about any of his opponents, about any of his fellow players.

In an era where rivalry carried a connotation of pit bulls going after each other with teeth bared, Borg actually was known to go out of his way to help other players. McEnroe often tells the story of how, mid-match, his temper had gotten the better of him, and Borg called him to the net and calmed him down before he could self-destruct.

That's how Borg was. I'm sure he'd give you the shirt off his back. I know for a fact he'd give you the shoes off his feet. He did it for me, literally, at Wimbledon in 1979.

For the two weeks that fall between the French Open and Wimbledon every year, the single mission of every touring professional is to adjust as quickly as possible from the red clay of Roland Garros to the slick grass courts in London. I was fortunate in 1979 to be able to practice every day during that time with Bjorn.

Adjusting to grass means many things. It means getting used to a different bounce and speed. For many players it means readjusting to the serve-and-volley style, hitting for winners instead of patiently working the point from the backcourt. But for every player the primary adjustment is footwork. Grass is just plain slippery.

Prior to 1980, most tennis shoes were pretty similar, at least as far as the undersole was concerned. And they were mostly useless on a grass court because they were flat, with little that would help a player gain traction on the slick green grass. Once or twice through the years someone named Laver or Roche or Rosewall might be allowed to wear short metal spikes (similar to those worn by track stars) in the finals of the U.S. Open, but the damage to the courts was too much to allow spikes to be worn throughout the tournament. In 1978 a company called Diadora changed grass court tennis forever.

Borg was under contract to Diadora, which produced a tennis shoe designed specifically for grass court play. It featured tiny "nubs" all over the sole of the shoe that offered a dramatically better grip on the grass. Interestingly, Diadora chose not to offer the shoes for sale—or even for anyone other than Borg. Borg had won the 1976 Wimbledon title wearing Adidas shoes. In 1977 and 1978 he was the only player in the draw to wear the new "grass court" Diadora shoes. In 1979 the company decided to offer the shoes to other Diadora contract players, such as Chris Lewis and John Alexander.

In 1979 I happened to be under contract to Nike, a company that had never made grass court shoes. As Borg and I practiced together regularly prior to Wimbledon, Borg gave me a pair of his Diadoras, just so that I could feel the difference. The difference was remarkable and I decided to wear them for the tournament. Of course I had to carefully "doctor" them every night in my hotel room to make sure nobody knew I was breaching my contract with Nike. I carefully unstitched the DIADORA logo and added the trademark Nike swoosh with a ballpoint pen, even adding the NIKE tab at the back of the shoe. Each day I'd wear my Nikes from the locker room out to the court, and then discreetly change before starting the warm-up. It was in Borg's shoes that I was able to reach the quarterfinals of Wimbledon that year. Naturally Borg won the title, his fourth in a row. Thereafter, Nike and every other shoe manufacturer provided the special "grass court shoes" to all of the players in the draw.

In July of 1980, Borg won his fifth Wimbledon title by defeating the twenty-one-year-old McEnroe in a classic Centre Court brawl. It was a five-set war. McEnroe slaughtered Borg in the first set, 6–1, but Borg rebounded and took the next two sets, 7–5 and 6–3. McEnroe won the fourth set 7–6 (18–16), a grueling thirty-four-point tiebreaker. Over the years I think every tennis fan I've ever spoken with has rated that tiebreaker as the most exciting fifteen minutes of tennis ever played. It had everything you could imagine all rolled into one minidrama: brilliant winners, horrible mistakes, match points, set points, and in the end McEnroe emerged victorious, leveling the match at two sets all. Borg, as you'd expect, barely shrugged his shoulders and never said a word as he changed ends to play the final set.

In *You Cannot Be Serious*, Mac's book written with James Kaplan, Mac wrote that after winning that fourth-set tiebreaker, "I knew I had won the match. Knew it." He knew wrong. Borg played what may very well have been the best set of his life and won, 8–6, to win his fifth consecutive Wimbledon singles title. No one knew until after the match that he had played with a torn stomach muscle.

THEIR RIVALRY WAS EPIC; the players were a study in contrast. That Wimbledon final was the eighth time that McEnroe, the hothead, and Borg, the cool Swede, had been across the net from each other. According to Borg, although McEnroe won their first meeting, an embarrassing 6–3, 6–4 loss in Sweden, their rivalry truly caught fire in the WCT Richmond match in 1979. McEnroe had eight match points and couldn't convert. Two weeks later in New Orleans, McEnroe turned the tables on Borg. Borg had five match points, but it was McEnroe who emerged triumphant. Two months after that, in the title match of the WCT Finals in Dallas, McEnroe won in a fourth-set tiebreaker.

The two couldn't have been more opposite. Their styles of play were diametrically opposed, McEnroe the classic serve-and-volleyer, Borg the perfect baseliner. Their personalities were even more dissimilar, from the way they treated people to the way they reacted to incidents on the court.

McEnroe had beaten Borg at the U.S. Open in 1980 for his second consecutive win in New York, but the breakthrough was in 1981 at Wimbledon. The torch officially passed when McEnroe finally took down the king of Wimbledon in a four-set final. After their performance the year before, the stage was set for another epic battle. It was an anticlimax. John played with his new Dunlop signature racket and used grass court shoes for the first time, proving finally that he had raised the bar just high enough to get past the legend.

The tennis viewing public was enjoying the best of all worlds. Here were two incredible talents, fire and ice, that met in every major final and clawed at each other for the top spot in the world rankings. Eight weeks later they were at it again in the final of the U.S. Open. How long could this go on? The fans looked forward to many more years of the same. It wasn't to be.

McEnroe won again in Louis Armstrong Stadium, his third U.S. title, and his third straight win over Borg in a major. Borg would never recover. Only he himself will ever know what was the final straw. Part of it may have been the aggravation of dealing with the MIPTC (Men's International Professional Tennis Council) over commitments to a full schedule. Part of it was that he had remained on top for so long that he couldn't continue to keep such a rigorous training schedule. A lot of it may have been that McEnroe just surpassed him. After all, Borg had been dominating the tennis world for several years before John even turned pro. Mac was just beginning his stride.

Whatever it was, Borg walked away. Retired. He would never play another Grand Slam event and the McEnroe–Borg rivalry was over.

HE WON THE ITALIAN OPEN twice and Wimbledon five times. He owned Roland Garros, winning it six times. Adrianno Panatta is the only player *ever* to beat Bjorn Borg at the French Open. But he was 0–10 at the U.S. Open and, like so many great champions, he left the game with one glaring omission. For Rosewall it was Wimbledon. Ditto Lendl. For Connors and McEnroe, the French.

SOME OF THE RIVALRIES that played out at that time were known mostly to the players on the tour and to real tennis fans; Vitas Gerulaitis and Wojtek Fibak never passed on the opportunity to take a "conversational run" at each other—off court or on. It's unclear how the two of them came to be such bad company; it just always seemed to be that way. However it started, their animosity grew exponentially over the years.

Gerulaitis refused to shake Fibak's hand in three straight tournaments and had called Fibak (among other unprintable things) a con man and a cheat. Fibak returned fire, calling Gerulaitis a spoiled American and a bad sport (along with a few unmentionables of his own). At one point Fibak tried to bury the hatchet after Gerulaitis beat him in five sets in the quarterfinals of the French Open in 1980. Vitas would have none of it. He responded that (for all intents and purposes) the only place he wanted to bury a hatchet was in Fibak's head. . . .

Fibak was not the most friendly guy on the tour. He rarely made much of an effort to socialize outside a very small group of friends—mostly nonplaying acquaintances scattered around Europe. I was not in that small group of friends. I mention this because it shocked the hell out of me when he phoned me the night before I was to play Gerulaitis in the finals of Zurich in 1982. The reason for his call? To give me all the information and guidance (strategy) he could offer on how to beat his enemy.

Most top players kept diaries or records of matches they played and notes on specific opponents. Fibak was no exception. More than most players, his was a game of finesse and strategy rather than brute force. He relied on knowing his opponent's weaknesses and how to exploit them. When Fibak opened his book to me, I was truly amazed. I still don't know what could inspire such hatred.

OTHER RIVALRIES WERE famous and infamous well outside the gates of the country clubs and regular tennis folk. These dragged players, officials, and fans alike into the mix, making it almost impossible to remain neutral. Connors–Borg. McEnroe–Borg. McEnroe–Connors. McEnroe–Lendl. Lendl–Connors. Even when the players tried to feign respect for each other in the press, no one believed for a minute that these two were going out for a few beers after the match.

When Borg abruptly announced his retirement, the tennis world was stunned, wondering what could take the place of the rivalry we'd seen develop between Borg and McEnroe.

CONNORS STEPPED UP to fill the void, with a little help from Ivan Lendl. Ivan had made his way up the ATP computer rankings in workmanlike fashion. He made it all the way to the top ten before he ever seriously contended in a major. The year 1982 is a good example. During the feud between Lamar Hunt's WCT Tour and the Grand Prix Tour operated by the MIPTC, Lendl chose to support WCT. He played thirteen events on that tour, including the WCT Finals in Dallas. He won them all. First prize was $100,000 in each and $150,000 for Dallas. Total take: $1,250,000. That's some Wheel of Fortune. But he finished the year ranked behind McEnroe and Connors. It wasn't that he didn't beat them, he just hadn't done it when it counted.

IN 1984 Mac had his finest year, probably the finest year any player has ever had. He won eighty-two matches and lost only three, but the year also marked one of his most disappointing losses. Borg's undoing was at Wimbledon in 1981. McEnroe's was at Roland Garros in 1984. One blemish on that near perfect record continues to haunt him. In the final of the French Open, he was up two sets to none and five points from taking the title. He lost in five sets to Ivan Lendl.

Ask me about Ivan Lendl and John McEnroe, and I'll tell you about the most personal rivalry in tennis's open era—off court and on. By the time of that fateful day when Lendl buried McEnroe in the cold red clay at Roland Garros, their encounters already numbered in the double digits. Lendl's victories already numbered in the double digits. Nevertheless, to this day John McEnroe insists he only lost the French because "he got tired." He'll never admit that he was simply outplayed. Rivalries don't work that way. To this day, McEnroe credits himself with making Ivan Lendl the great champion he was—revisionist history at its finest.

McEnroe once said of Lendl: "I have more personality up my ass." While I'm probably the last guy who should comment on what McEnroe does or does not have up his ass I will say this: Lendl was doing a pretty good job of letting his forehand fill the room with personality.

McEnroe also said of Lendl: "I have more talent in my little finger than he has in his entire body." Yeah, okay, Mac was a tennis genius. Talent certainly was one of the things McEnroe had a load of up his ol' wazoo, but let the record show: Lendl won more Grand Slam titles than McEnroe. McEnroe was the game's number-one player for four years until his defeat at the hands of Lendl at the U.S. Open in 1985. Lendl held that number-one position for 270 weeks—five full years. In their rivalry, Lendl would best McEnroe twenty-one times.

Besting McEnroe even extended to Lendl's dreams. Once when we were practicing together at his home in Connecticut, Ivan told me he actually woke up laughing that morning. What had been so funny? He had dreamed he was playing Mac in Dallas and had hit him so hard with the ball at close range that Mac fell on his— well, you know.

Mac publicly took Lendl to task for his penchant of aiming balls directly at him. "That just shows what a classy person he is," McEnroe told a reporter. "I have no respect for anyone who would go out of their way to hit a player." (Allow me to pause one moment to choke on that little piece of hypocrisy).

Lendl's *classy* response? "It's against the rules to hit him with my fists."

When Lendl was seeking U.S. citizenship, there were some who speculated that he and Mac might become Davis Cup teammates. Mac, who had managed somehow to team with Connors (no one said it went well, but at least it went), said, "That would be difficult for me to swallow."

Lendl, nonplussed, shot back, "It's hard to imagine anyone with his mouth having a difficult time swallowing anything." Seriously.

As Lendl's friend and doubles partner, I was all too aware of his "feelings" for McEnroe—it was something we had in common, for there was one McEnroe rivalry I was even more familiar with. Mine.

Now, don't misunderstand, I've never imagined myself to be in the same league of champions as Lendl, Connors, McEnroe, or any of the others, but it's my book, so . . .

3:

MAC AND ME

OKAY, I HAVE TO GET into the "relationship" between John McEnroe and myself. I know this book is not supposed to be about me but, honestly, one of the best insights I can share with you from my years in pro tennis is the opportunity to lock horns in an ongoing feud with one of the best players of all time.

My very first knowledge of John was at his stomping grounds, the Port Washington Tennis Academy in New York, and our scheduled junior tournament match. I think I was sixteen, so he must have been thirteen or fourteen and playing up in the older division, a testament to his considerable talent.

We were just a couple of kids, but we both were absolutely certain of what we wanted to be when we grew up. Some kids dreamed of being an astronaut or a fireman. For John McEnroe and myself, Rod Laver was the role model. We wanted to be tennis players, and Laver was the best the world had ever known.

At the Port Washington Tennis Academy that day, I was leading handily in the first set when McEnroe suddenly decided to quit. He simply walked off the court—defaulted. No explanation or even any great drama. He just left. I never knew why and didn't give it a lot of thought at the time, but I suppose it was a portent of things to come. It was a sign of one thing for certain; he didn't take losing graciously. Without a word, he had simply quit.

It wouldn't be the last time his behavior would defy my comprehension. Little did my teenaged self know that John and I were to spend many years aggravating each other.

The first time I played John as a pro, he was still an amateur. We played in the doubles final in Ocean City, Maryland, in a tournament on the entrepreneurial Riordan–Scott circuit in February of 1977. He was paired with Cliff Richey, a fellow Texan of mine, and I was paired with Alex Metreveli.

Tennis was Cliff Richey's life. He barely escaped high school and didn't even consider college. His focus was squarely set on one thing and that was tennis. It paid off. Richey earned the number-one ranking in the United States in 1970—amazingly the same year his sister, Nancy, was also ranked the number-one female player in America. Long before his doubles partner that day made the practice vogue, Cliff Richey had an established reputation as a poster boy for bad behavior.

Amateur McEnroe had only just begun to pick up that little nuance.

Alex Metreveli, my partner that day, was a terrific Russian player. He had been Wimbledon finalist in 1973, the year of the players' strike, the infamous all-Communist final. In February of 1977, his impressive career was winding down. Me? I was at the beginning of my first full year as a pro, the up-and-comer.

What I remember most about the match, amazingly, is that I have absolutely no recollection of it at all. I've been told that it occurred. A friend sent me a newspaper clipping about the match. There are records to show that it was my first professional encounter with McEnroe, but I don't remember it at all. I guess it's not so very important that I remember; the important thing is that Metreveli and I won the doubles title. We split a whoppin' $2,000.

John would make a much larger impression on me, and everybody else, at Wimbledon later that year, making a great run all the way through the qualifying rounds to reach the semifinals. There he lost to Jimmy Connors. Like a lot of people, I was surprised that he chose not to turn pro immediately but elected to attend Stanford for a year, winning the NCAA title in 1978, two years after I had done the same.

From the first day that he arrived on the tour, John seemed to have a problem with me. I never knew why, but since he seemed to have problems with a lot of guys, I never took it personally. Years later when I read *You Cannot Be Serious,* I was surprised by a reference John made to our times together as roommates traveling on the Junior Davis Cup team. He explained that since we had been friendly on that junior tour, he was hurt and insulted by my indifference to him when he joined the pro ranks. He even suggested that I had made a comment along the lines of "We were never friends in the juniors." I can certainly understand his disappointment except for one minor detail: As a junior player I never qualified for the Junior Davis Cup team and clearly we never traveled together as roommates. I just wasn't there. I have no idea who he recalls being friendly with, but it wasn't me. It's strange to think that all these years of animosity might have been based on a case of mistaken identity.

Late in 1978, John and I met in the semifinals of the Island Holidays Classic in Maui. The year had been a difficult one for me. After a year and a half on the tour, a lot of the players had figured out my game and were less intimidated by me as a player. I had also struggled with a new racket that Fila was attempting to make for me. I was lured by a potentially large contract and the company promised me that the Fila Bill Scanlon Autograph racket would be a copy of the Jack Kramer Autograph that I had used for years. Unfortunately, they were never able to make it feel the same. We went through countless prototypes and the net effect was that eventually I lost confidence in all of them and even had difficulty going back to my old Kramers.

By the fall of the year, my ranking had slipped so far that I even had to qualify for the Maui event. Mac was just the opposite. He was the bright new star ascending. The computer had the rookie ranked fifth in the world, and he already had a couple of titles under his belt. When we met in the semifinals, I was older and had more experience, but not the kind of experience you like to have. I was clearly the underdog, hardly expected to beat the great McEnroe.

Certainly we knew each other by the time we met in Maui, and I was aware of John's reputation, but Maui was my first real experience with his repertoire of "tactics." Over the years it became pretty well accepted that most of John's tantrums, arguments, and so on, would take place when he was struggling in a match or when his opponent was on a hot streak. We all knew that his strategy was to cause a distraction or force a delay so that his opponent would lose concentration, maybe even get angry that his good play was being interrupted.

The first player I remember getting vocal about John's tactics was Sandy Mayer, a top ten player and 1973 Stanford NCAA champion in singles and doubles. Mac had stalled so many times to tie his shoes during one of their matches that Sandy loudly volunteered to come across the net and tie them permanently for him. No one really believes that John's shoes were really such a problem—or even that he needed more time between points to psych himself up. He just knew that Sandy had a "by the book" type of personality and would get annoyed if John stretched the rules and got away with it. He was right. Sandy even carried his primary complaint ("McEnroe shouldn't be doing that") into the press conference after the match.

In Maui I got my first taste of what was to become a steady diet of Mac stew. Though I've never considered myself to be in the same league as John in terms of rankings or major results, I enjoyed a record against him that was better than would be expected for a player of my ranking. It just happened that my game was well suited to playing him. His convoluted serve never bothered me as much as it did other players, and he rarely managed to overpower me effectively.

Additionally, I was coached from day one to take advantage of John's "creative genius" by forcing him to be repetitive against his nature. Bob Mooty, my very first tennis instructor who also coached me throughout my career, suggested that I imagine John trying to hit backhand crosscourt drills for twenty minutes. It would have driven him crazy! Bob's suggestion was that when I played John I should keep hitting to the same spot over and over. "Make him do exactly what he hates to do!" I have to say there were times when it worked really well. It was even better when John realized what I was doing and that made him even more crazy.

One more thing helped me to play better against McEnroe than lots of players at my level (or even higher). I believed from the very beginning that all of McEnroe's tantrums were contrived and, as I've said, tactics that he would use in competition with an opponent who was playing well. For that reason I never approached the situation thinking, *He shouldn't be doing this. He's upsetting my rhythm.* Rather, my attitude was: *This is one of the weapons he has — just like his serve or his backhand — that I need to overcome.* In a strange way I was almost flattered that John needed to use it so frequently against me.

The good news for me is that over the years my tactics were often successful against McEnroe, despite my lower ranking. The bad news is that this really pissed him off. I'm sure he never enjoyed struggling with a player he considered to be below his stature, and that's probably why I got pretty frequent doses of the famous McEnroe tantrums. Maui was no exception.

Bad news: My best friend, Richard Peyton, had a party at his home, where I just happened to be staying the night before the match. Richard was the head pro at the Royal Lahaina Tennis Ranch, the site of the tournament and was well connected in the town. Knowing how uncertain my career was at this point,

Richard had spent the entire week practicing with me and enlisting friends (and friends of friends) to support me in my matches. Anyway, at the party that night a mutual friend, Bill Chaffee, gave an inspiring pep talk. He referred to a recently released movie, *The Bad News Bears*, which, ironically enough, starred Tatum O'Neal. In front of about forty friends Bill rambled on and finally wound up his speech by saying, "Tomorrow Scanlon plays McEnroe, and you know what that means?" An entire room of well-wishers shouted as one, "Bad News for McEnroe!"

Of course none of us had any idea that, years later, Mac would marry the movie's child star—bad news for both of them.

Mac pulled every trick in the book that day. Every time I played well for a stretch, he would argue line calls, berate linesmen, and have long arguments with the umpire. It seemed the only time he was quiet was when he was winning handily.

Time and again I found myself standing around waiting for him to continue play. Fortunately for me, I was surrounded in the stands by Richard and the newly formed gang of supporters, so I kept my concentration and never really got bothered or upset. Through all the tantrums, delays, and arguments, I finally managed to win in three long sets.

Later that night, my friend Richard gave Mac a dose of his own stall-and-delay tactics. As our group of friends was getting settled for dinner at a restaurant called the Ocean House in Lahaina, Richard called my attention to the front door where McEnroe was arriving for dinner with a few friends. Richard excused himself for a few minutes and, on his return, he volunteered that he had spoken with the manager of the restaurant, a friend, and was assured that McEnroe's wait for a table would be a long one. As we left the restaurant, they had still not been seated.

AUTHOR'S NOTE: After beating McEnroe in the semifinals, I went on to play Peter Fleming in the finals. In *You Cannot Be Serious*, McEnroe referred to my match in the finals against Fleming, *his* best friend and doubles partner. He said that he actually hoped that I would win so that he (McEnroe) would look better by comparison. Having been eliminated, it was important to him to have lost to the titleist. He wasn't in the stands supporting his friend, instead opting to wait in the hotel room to learn the results.

Mac got his wish that day. I beat Fleming in the finals, 6–2, 6–0. With friends like that . . .

In early 1981, I played Mac in Los Angeles at the L.A. Tennis Club. My guest for the semifinal night match was Irving Azoff, megamusic manager of the Eagles and various other superstars. I was staying at Irving's home in Beverly Hills with his wife, Shelli, and their toddlers, Jennifer and Allison. The Azoffs and I had spent great times together as they traveled with me to tournaments in Maui, Las Vegas, and New York City.

McEnroe and I were, to put it nicely, less than civil to each other at that time and Irving loved to stir up the rivalry. No stranger to conflict, he would goad me on and encourage me to have fun with the battle. Our match in Los Angeles would make Irving very proud.

During one of the changeovers, Mac and I reached the net-post at the same time, heads down and walking purposefully. Neither of us gave ground, and we collided almost head-on right in front of the umpire's chair. The crowd howled, and above it all I could hear Irving shrieking with laughter.

I didn't win that match, but later that night when we went to a recording studio for Stevie Nicks's recording session, Irving must have told the story a dozen times, each more exaggerated and animated than the last.

In later years Irving would become friendly with McEnroe, partnering for a series of successful exhibition matches—almost a tennis rock 'n' roll tour. I felt totally betrayed at the time and backed off from my friendship with the Azoffs. Time, maturity, and perspective have prevailed, though, and these days Irving and I see each other frequently, sharing a passion for golf and skiing. He eventually retained me for financial services for himself and a client, Don Henley of the Eagles. I have no idea if Irving and John are still friends—somehow the subject never seems to come up.

Toward the end of 1981, a couple of months after our strange encounter in San Francisco, John's on-court antics elevated again.

At the Seiko Super Challenge in Tokyo, John was fined for "abuse of an opponent" during a match. Surprise: It just happened to be me again. This time, though, I finally learned a little about what was going on in his head. During the course of this outburst (to the total confusion of the umpire and everyone else), John rambled on about what had happened in San Francisco two months earlier. While I was baffled by his impromptu lecture at the Cow Palace, Mac was obsessed with what had happened last—my removal of the point penalties. While I thought I had done the decent thing—the sportsmanlike thing—in having the point penalties removed, Mac didn't quite see it the same way. His view was that I had "made him look bad."

One bitter rival showing up the other. That's what Mac thought I had done to him, and he had entered the match in Tokyo determined to make me pay one way or the other.

I don't even remember for certain how it started this time, except that Mac disagreed with a line call and was going to share his viewpoint with the umpire. Apparently his viewpoint was that I was an asshole because I "made him look bad." Therefore, I was responsible for the bad call and any number of other problems that John was experiencing.

The umpire's viewpoint was that McEnroe's viewpoint constituted an "abuse of an opponent." There is a penalty associated with that ruling and this didn't help John's mood at all.

It didn't end there. After the match, which he won, 6–4/6–3, Mac walked off the court without shaking my hand. A mostly Japanese audience steeped in a culture of honor sat in stunned silence when Mac left the court. When I left, they gave me a standing ovation. I guess Mac thought he had given me my comeuppance; that he was teaching me some sort of lesson. I'm really not sure what he was thinking, and I half expected some kind of exchange in the locker room afterward, but John left immediately after his press conference without showering.

Mac found out about his fines the next day just before his match with Vince van Patten. I only thought he had gone off on me the day before. Supervisor Bill Gilmour really got an earful, as did anyone within a half-mile radius. It was Richter scale stuff. Mac not only was riled that he had been fined, but more concerned with the fact that I hadn't been. I'm not sure what it was I was supposed to have done to deserve a fine, but that's Mac.

He worked himself into such a froth that he wasn't really even competitive against van Patten. Vinnie is no stranger to big matches and was always dangerous against top opponents such as Mac or Connors, especially in a showcase match. On this day he brought his "A" game and McEnroe spent another afternoon being miserable. Vinnie is another player who isn't particularly fond of John's tactics and at the end of their match Vinnie gave Mac the old "fake-out" handshake. . . .

What had happened in Tokyo was the talk of the press and the talk among players for some time. It was the fourth time we had played each other in six months, and things between us had progressed from bad to worse.

In two other matches against John, I held match points and failed to convert. One was in San Jose, California, in 1979. The other is possibly the most gut-wrenching loss of my career. In our first battle since Tokyo, we were on my turf. I played career tennis for four hours and forty minutes and managed to hold four match points before losing in front of my hometown crowd of nineteen thousand people at the 1982 WCT Finals in Dallas. I staved off fourteen break points, but I couldn't convert when I really needed to. It seemed that my greatest adversary wasn't John McEnroe, but myself. I lost the fourth match point on an unforced error. The match didn't end until well after midnight. Emotionally, I was totally torn up over the loss. Physically, I was so sore I could barely move for days.

The match set a record for the longest match in WCT history as I went down, 6–4, in the fifth after dropping the fourth-set tiebreak, 10–8. None of the games had been runaways. That match was a testament to the fact that as much as neither John nor I wanted to lose, we most definitely didn't want to lose to each other.

I think just about everyone watching at Reunion Arena wanted me to win, with the possible exception of Lamar Hunt, who understandably wanted a revenue-generating Lendl–McEnroe final (which he got and which Lendl won).

By 1983 I was playing the best tennis of my career. I was traveling with Warren Jacques, who also coached Steve Denton and Kevin Curren, and he had whipped my game into shape. I had broken into the top twenty of the rankings, reaching four finals and about eight semis over a few months' stretch. Arriving at Wimbledon, I was in full stride, totally confident. Seeded fourteenth in the event, I saw that I was scheduled to meet McEnroe in the round of sixteen if we both got there. I was psyched because I knew I had a chance to beat him.

When the match arrived we were scheduled for Center Court and the conditions were perfect. I believe I played some of my best tennis that day and still lost—straight sets, 7–5, 7–6, 7–6. The match lasted more than three hours. Even the tiebreaks weren't runaways. They went to 9–7. Unfortunately, they went to Mac.

It was probably the highest level of tennis, from a skills point of view, that McEnroe and I ever played against each other. Not coming out on top was emotionally devastating. I was crushed. I knew that I had a chance. I had brought my best tennis. It simply wasn't good enough.

Bob Mooty tried to encourage me afterward by pointing out that although I had lost in straight sets, I had held set point in each of the three sets. Three points was all that separated me from the best player in the world and a possible Wimbledon title. Mac won the Wimbledon title easily, beating Chris Lewis in the final, 6–2, 6–2, 6–2.

Three points! Bob Mooty kept reminding me all summer. We practiced for six hours a day, every day. We even practiced tiebreaks on a daily basis. In every one of those practices, I pretended I was playing McEnroe and I would think to myself, *Three points*. It proved to be very valuable encouragement eight weeks later.

At the U.S. Open in August, I entered the tournament as the sixteenth seed. Guess who I was scheduled to meet in the round of sixteen if we both got there? It was an added incentive that drove me through three rounds to reach each other yet again.

In retrospect, I should say that my looking ahead to McEnroe was perhaps somewhat ambitious. Because I was so focused on the chance to play Mac again, I barely noticed that my road to meet him would go through Henrik Sundstrom (top ten), Chris Lewis (Wimbledon finalist), and Pat Cash (Wimbledon champion).

The appointed hour was Labor Day, Monday, round of sixteen.

Mac's day got off to a bad start when he was denied entrance to the players' parking lot. At his most truculent, Mac demanded of the parking attendant: "Don't you know who I am?" Believe it or not, the guy didn't. "Why don't you show me your driver's license and then we'll both know" was the man's response. Of course, eventually Mac was allowed to park his car, but his day didn't get any better. In no small part, that was due to me.

We played the feature match on center court at Flushing Meadows on Monday afternoon, Labor Day. Full house, national TV. I practiced with Jimmy Connors the day before, probably one of the few times he's ever offered anything constructive. The opportunity to practice with a left-hander proved to be invaluable.

Our last two sets at Wimbledon had been tiebreakers, and our first two sets at the U.S. Open were tiebreakers as well. All I could think was: *Three points*. It was like a mantra, over and over: *Three points*. Every time Mac would start an argument with the umpire, I would retreat to the corner of the court and think: *Three points, three points*.

The arguments started early. I was serving, down 5–6 in the first set, and Mac objected to a call that gave me 30-all. When I went on to hold serve, taking the first set to a tiebreak, Mac refused to serve and was given a warning by our chair umpire,

Ken Slye. Mac decided it was time for an up close and personal conversation with the chair. I just stood in the corner thinking: *Three points*.

The tiebreak went my way, 7–2. The second set went to a tiebreak as well, and three spectators were ejected at Mac's "request." They were disturbing him. I was disturbing him, too. Mac nearly decapitated me with an overhead smash, but he missed and I won the second-set tiebreak, 7–2.

Mac won the third set, and the fourth set became open warfare. From the net he fired a shot straight at my head, sending me into evasive maneuvers. We had a thing or two to say to each other. A couple of points later, he did connect aiming for my gut. Luckily, I swiveled away in time to catch it in the hip instead. The thought of retaliating in kind crossed my mind briefly, but I just turned my game up a notch instead.

The New York crowd had turned on the New York kid and were loudly pulling for me. Mac again delayed the match, expressing displeasure to Slye, then took to his chair, once again refusing to play. *Three points,* I told myself.

Mac pulled ahead two games to one and had me triple break point, then I just went on a tear and had Mac down, 5–3. He went up, 40–15, and we were both giving it all we had to give. There had been stares and glares and words exchanged all through the match, but it had finally come to a head.

I held match point with Mac serving. All I could hear was this whisper in my head: *Three points*. Single fault. *Three points*. When he fired his second serve, I was waiting for it with my backhand and I nailed it down the line for a winner.

I erupted and the crowd erupted. Mac was strangely quiet.

During the match, Mike Lupica compared us to a couple of welterweight boxers—"Boom Boom Scanlon" and "Sugar Ray McEnroe"—and speculated whether we would shake hands at the end of the match (we did). John Newcombe said he was going to avoid the locker room in case we came to blows (we didn't).

The newspapers had a field day with their headlines the next day. My favorite was a *New York Post* edition that showed a photo of Mac with his head hung low and a headline that said: BYE BYE BRAT.

For all my relief at getting the win, I still had a tournament to play. I had a hard time focusing on my next match because of all the attention—even the general manager of my hotel called to offer me the presidential suite at no charge and use of the hotel limousine.

On Wednesday night, after one day off, I faced Mark Dickson in the quarterfinals. The match drew very little attention but was very satisfying for me. One of the toughest things to do is to come back after a big win and stay focused for the next round. Mark had made a good run to the quarterfinals and was a young player with lots of talent. I had also lost to him a couple of times. Our match lasted four and a half hours, ending well after midnight as I won in a tiebreaker in the fifth set.

On Super Saturday my ride finally came to an end as I faced my most difficult opponent of the tournament: Jimmy Connors. Once before I had faced Jimmy in a big match: the quarterfinals of Wimbledon. It was my first chance to make a breakthrough in a major and I had gotten off to a good start. At one set all, I managed to lead, five games to two, in the third set. I was playing well and started to imagine beating Connors in four sets. Lesson Number One in tennis: Don't get ahead of yourself, especially against Connors. I choked.

Jimmy came back to win the set in a tiebreaker and then closed me out in a fairly routine fourth set. At the U.S. Open in 1983 I was determined not to make the same mistake. Now, anyone who follows tennis knows that Jimmy Connors is a different player at the U.S. Open than anywhere else in the world. There is an energy in the stadium that is unique and Jimmy feeds on it like a shark in bloody waters.

As much as I prepared for the match, it was my first time in the semifinals of a major and I was overwhelmed by the situation. I don't recall ever being so nervous. Having worked so hard to get back into the top twenty, I now had secured a place in the top ten for the first time in my career and was fully aware that a win over Connors could change my entire career, put me up a notch or two. Unfortunately, I never got into the match. I lost in three straight sets and left New York feeling great that I had reached the semis.

McEnroe and I were not through with our ongoing feud. Fast-forward to next year's Wimbledon. We had played each other once since the Open, in Madrid in March. We had a tiebreak, and I had set point, but he came out on top.

In 1984 John was having his best year of tennis ever. He had played devastating tennis against everyone, his only loss to Ivan Lendl at the French Open. He had won forty-two straight matches until that fifth-set loss. He really seemed invincible. My ranking had once again reached the top ten. Again I was seeded fourteenth at Wimbledon and again we were scheduled to meet in the round of sixteen if we both got there.

The papers built it up as they always do in London, though I sincerely tried to avoid reading them. Before the first round had even been played, they had me pegged as the one person who could rattle him—off court and on.

After I beat Boris Becker and he beat Wally Masur in the third round, the press kicked into high gear. In our post-match press conferences Saturday, neither of us was asked about what had happened in the third round, but about what was going to happen in the fourth round.

Amazingly, the press even had John linked romantically to a fashion model that I had dated several years earlier. I have no idea if it was true, but it really went over the top. Our rivalry had turned into tabloid fodder. It was going to be a long weekend.

Wimbledon officials had a meeting the night before our match. What would they do if there was trouble? They went so far as to actually take out an insurance policy with Lloyds of London in case the tournament lost money because of the default of a top player.

McEnroe had not exploded yet during the tournament, but the

storm flags were raised now. Arthur Ashe called it "the match to see" and reminded everyone of what had happened in Tokyo. An hour before the match, the touts (ticket scalpers) were getting £200 apiece (about $270) for our match on Court One. By comparison, the tickets for Lendl's match on Centre Court that day were only getting £70. Everyone expected quite a show.

Unfortunately, the match failed to live up to the hype. Mac played the best I had ever seen him play. I really never managed to put up a fight and lost in straight sets.

It would be two and a half years until I faced Mac across a net again. It hadn't been the best of times for Mac or me. For myself, I spent 1985 dealing with two knee surgeries. For John, I can't honestly say I know for sure where the problems started, but I do know that he wasn't living up to his normal, very high standards.

To rebuild my game and my legs after the surgeries, I had spent a great deal of time training with Ivan Lendl at his home in Greenwich, and his work ethic had really rubbed off on me. We played a number of doubles tournaments together and in February 1987 we entered the Lipton Championships in Key Biscayne, Florida.

We had won a doubles title the month before in Australia and now we were about to be tested against the best doubles team ever: McEnroe and . . .

I don't know where Peter Fleming was that day, but John was paired with Matt Mitchell, his former Stanford teammate. John wasn't playing singles in the tournament because he'd had wisdom teeth pulled and was in foul humor, even by his salty standards.

Two bitter rivals staring Mac down. The match was—well, let's just say it was interesting. After we won the first set, 6–4, Mac started mouthing off to umpire Rich Kaufman about his lousy officiating. Clearly we had gotten under his skin. He was I-rate.

The second set was a world war. Mac and Matt took it, 7–6 (7–5), and Ivan was I-rate. He was absolutely convinced the officials were favoring Mac.

In the third set, he let Mac get under his skin, and he started choking the match away. I was I-rate.

I had to pull Lendl aside for a little one-on-one sports psychology. All I could think to do was to tell him he was dead right.

What I told Ivan was this: Of course the officials were favoring McEnroe. John wasn't in the singles and the tournament promoters desperately needed to keep him in the event for marquee value. The match was rigged to keep the gate attraction in the tournament. Duh. Now, wouldn't it be fun to screw up their little plan?

Ivan bought it and his game was transformed.

At one point he fired such an intense whipping forehand right at McEnroe that Mac had to dive for cover. Lendl was dead serious in his intent, and it was all I could do to keep a straight face.

In the third game of the third set, everything hit the fan. Lendl was serving to John in the Ad court. McEnroe thought the serve hit the net, but no call was made and he went into another one of his tirades, a pretty good one by my estimation, and I had witnessed a lot of them. In the world according to Mac, everyone in the stadium had seen and heard the ball hit the net *except* the umpire. John had Rich Kaufman practically under siege in his chair, screaming like some strung-out banshee.

John was cited for two conduct violations and fined heavily for the things he said and did in that meltdown. Ivan and I went on to win the match.

For over a decade, I had gone head to head with one of the best players in the history of our game. Our "relationship" had been bitter, intense, and fiery. Still, retrospect is a funny thing and twenty years later my perspective is this: I played with the best. I gave him fits, even managed to win a few. It's fun to have played a small part in the greatest era of tennis's history.

4:

EQUIPMENT MATTERS

IN LOS ANGELES former tour player Ron Hightower keeps a collection of tennis rackets extending back to the turn of the century. It is a fascinating journey through the decades of competitive tennis. The collection is also a curious expression of what players found to be the most effective tools of their craft combined with what the sporting goods manufacturers felt they could market profitably to consumers.

It was in the '30s that the world embraced a common size and shape of wooden racket that would endure virtually unchanged until the late '60s. The only distinguishing characteristics of competing brands and models were largely cosmetic for marketing purposes.

Because most tennis rackets were designed to be almost identical in length, width, and head shape, brand identity was achieved most often by attaching a top player's signature to the model. Companies would aggressively recruit top players and offer them free equipment in return for the player's endorsement of the racket. In the days of amateur tennis, the free equipment was the extent of a player's marketability. Professionals during that era were actually paid to use the rackets in match play and to act as spokesmen for the company. It came to be rather a status symbol over the years to have a racket named for you. Well-known signature models of our generation included the Stan Smith, Guillermo Vilas, Chris Evert, Bjorn Borg, and Vitas Gerulaitis. Earlier models were named for Laver, Emerson, Rosewall, Gonzalez, and a host of other players who were champions through the years.

The most notable and successful of the signature rackets that were marketed in this century was without a doubt the Jack Kramer Autograph offered by Wilson Sporting Goods in the United States. The racket, named for tour legend Jack Kramer, was so popular among competitive tour players and social weekend players that it was offered in at least three versions: the original, the Jack Kramer Pro Staff, and the Kramer Autograph Pro Select.

Although Wilson's marketing department never admitted the fact (and probably wouldn't even today), most players who tried the rackets agreed that, except for cosmetics, the rackets were virtually indistinguishable. The only difference between any of them was the cosmetic markings, such as the color of the plastic trim or the stain of the wood. The Pro Staff had small wooden diamond inserts laid into the fiberglass faceplate that had absolutely no effect on the playability of the racket. I used all three at one time or another and I'm sure that I could never have passed a blind test.

The success of the Kramer Autograph continued long past the normal time span that companies expected for a typical branded frame, so the executives at Wilson decided to take advantage of their good fortune. Their plan was sheer marketing genius: They took the original frame, added a longer strip of wood along the handle running up the faceplate, changed the colors of the decals, and, with new artwork, offered virtually the same racket as the "new" Stan Smith Autograph, the Chris Evert Autograph, and the Billie Jean King Autograph, and so on. To be fair, the "new" frames did actually feel slightly stiffer than the original because of the thicker, shored-up throat.

Other companies made various attempts to attract market share by offering slightly modified versions of a popular racket. The Dunlop Maxfli was probably the second-most popular frame on the market in the United States. It was played by Rod Laver and a host of other pros. When Laver renegotiated his endorsement contract with Dunlop, he agreed to play and promote the Rod Laver Elite Dunlop racket. Naturally it was the exact same frame as the Maxfli. New decals and a darker stain on the wood were the "new improvements."

Interestingly, the original Maxfli was offered in several different varieties that were, in fact, structurally *different* without name changes. The official explanation from company representatives was that frames were manufactured in different countries, for different countries, according to different specs. One actually had a smaller, rounder head than the original. Another was one-half inch shorter than the rest. Very interesting choices when one considers that eventually the trend in rackets would go in exactly the opposite directions.

As tennis boomed in the mid-'70s, racket sales were increasing dramatically. Companies were extremely eager to cash in on the bonanza and produced countless "new, improved" frames for the public to buy. The good news was that wooden rackets had a limited life span. After a while they would break, warp, or simply go soft. Temper tantrums were encouraged by the manufacturers— they invested heavily in Nastase and McEnroe—because replacements were big business.

The higher level of play, the greater the sensitivity to the playing characteristics of the rackets. The problem of wooden rackets going soft was the primary reason that professionals would go through so many frames. I'm sure each player was different, but my experience with the Kramers was that I could expect about three good weeks of play from a new frame. Remember, we played three to five hours a day, with considerable power forced onto the head of the racket. I averaged about eighty-five total hours before needing a replacement. Kevin Curren, who used the Kramer Pro Staff, might have weakened his frames even sooner because of his considerably harder serve. It was common for tour players to travel with ten or twelve rackets each week on the tour.

The problem for manufacturers trying to sell more rackets was that most of the rackets were all basically similar, and social players could barely tell the difference between them. The need for brand identity was greater than ever and this led to more signature brands. In the '70s they were everywhere, primarily because the companies had very little to lose. They would usually come up with new cosmetics for an existing frame, add a player's name, and *presto*: the Fila Bill Scanlon Autograph tennis racket.

A LITTLE-KNOWN FACT of the late '70s is that tour players, eager to cash in on their newfound marketability, would sign contracts to endorse signature rackets while actually playing in tournaments with a racket of their preferred brand that had been painted over to look like their signature brand—the "fine art" of racket disguise.

Remember, players tended to get attached to certain rackets. Perhaps it was superstition, or maybe familiarity, but players would adjust to the racket they liked and begin to feel as though the racket became a natural extension of their arm. Feel and touch were a big part of the game in those years and players rarely would want to risk losing that feel by using an unfamiliar racket. On the subject of endorsement, the conventional wisdom was that a player should never risk his ranking just to get a bigger racket contract. "The money you earn by winning just one tournament with the racket you like could make up for the amount you might get from a contract. And if your game goes bad, well . . ."

The money was so attractive, though, that enterprising minds (and maybe their agents) came up with a way for players to "have their cake and eat it too." The manufacturers played along.

Ilie Nastase signed a big-money endorsement contract to use Adidas shoes, clothing, and the new Ilie Nastase Autograph Adidas racket—which he didn't even use. In fact, Adidas wasn't really in the racket-manufacturing business, so they didn't really have a frame available for him to use. The rackets they sold were manufactured elsewhere and "private-labeled" to specs provided by the company. None of these were professional-quality frames, so Ilie chose to "Picasso" the racket frame he actually used, the Stan Smith Autograph.

Later versions of the same story were carried out with slightly more integrity. When Ivan Lendl signed a contract with Adidas approximately ten years later, it was similar to Nastase's arrangement in that it was an "all-products" deal. He had been using a Kneisl midsized frame manufactured in Austria. Ranked number one in the world, Ivan wasn't about to switch rackets, and he definitely wasn't about to risk his credibility by deceiving the public. The solution? Adidas bought the manufacturing plant in Austria and the rights to produce the frame from Kneisl. Adidas designs were added and a new product line was born.

Bjorn Borg took brand identity to an even higher level. Borg's agents, Bob Kain and IMG, negotiated a monster endorsement contract for Bjorn to use and promote the Donnay racket in the late '70s. Interestingly, Donnay never had a distribution capability in the United States and, thus, never marketed the racket used by the Wimbledon champion in the largest sports market in the world. Never one to miss an opportunity, Kain arranged for Borg's Donnay contract to exclude the United States. He was free to make other arrangements, which he did with a great old company, Bancroft. Both were, of course, Bjorn Borg Autograph (signature) rackets, with marketing campaigns designed to maximize the association the world's number-one player at that time. I don't think anyone would be surprised to learn that Borg actually used the same frames regardless of where he played in the world. Only the cosmetics were changed.

Borg commanded more special attention than any player of the era. This is true with respect to many different issues, one of them being his equipment. Most players received rackets from the manufacturers that were selected according to their identical weight, balance, and possibly flex. This was a common practice because it was important for players to have the same feel from one frame to the next. Even so, all of the rackets were stock issue, meaning they were culled from the same production lines that went for purchase by the general public. It was possible for any club player to purchase an exact copy of John McEnroe's Pro Staff or Jimmy Connors's Wilson T2000. Borg's Donnays and Bancrofts were different.

As was the case with his Wimbledon "grass court shoes," Bjorn Borg played with tennis rackets that were manufactured specially for him and not offered to anyone else. Not for other Donnay contract players, not for sale to the general public. First, the rackets weighed in at over fifteen ounces, a weight that was virtually useless for social players. Because of his two-handed backhand, Borg also played with an extended "Fairway" brand grip that ran almost halfway up the throat of the racket.

Most importantly, the head of Bjorn's personal rackets was reinforced with extra layers of fiberglass to increase stiffness. This also helped the frame to support the eighty-plus pounds of string tension that Borg made his trademark. Most normal frames would collapse in a matter of hours under that stress. On the occasions when a string would break in one of Bjorn's rackets, the frame could be seen to contort due to the now-unequal pressure on the wood. It was Borg's habit (with the help of Lennart Bergelin) to travel with sixty to eighty rackets at any given time, because bunches of them were constantly being restrung.

WHEN WILSON SPORTING GOODS introduced the T2000 open-throated racket that would become the magic wand used by Jimmy Connors, the tennis world gasped at the novel design. A couple of smaller companies had tried to introduce similar frames (Tensor comes to mind) with little success, but when the tennis powerhouse Wilson Sporting Goods, with all its marketing clout, made a major commitment to the market, the game took notice. Billie Jean King had used the frame, as did Clark Graebner, but it was Connors who got the world talking about the revolution. Surprise.

After the twenty-two-year-old Connors used his metal racket to slaughter a Slazenger wood-bearing (and thirty-nine-year-old) Ken Rosewall in the 1974 Wimbledon and U.S. Open finals, the T2000 became the first racker to successfully alter the public perception of what a tennis racket should be, and it started a landslide. It was closely followed by numerous innovations such as Head's Pro Model, Master Model, and even Arthur Ashe's Head Competition, and the field was now wide open for whatever improvements the imagination could yield.

In fact, a trip through Ron Hightower's collection would have shocked many current players and fans who were so taken by the "new" developments in equipment. Open-throated and even steel frames had been used fifty and sixty years before. One of the more curious innovations of those early times was the use of steel (wire) strings rather than the customary gut or nylon.

The revolution of the '70s yielded a great range of marketing efforts. Round heads, rectangle heads, off-set heads, I even saw a racket with a wide head that could accommodate two sets of strings about a quarter of an inch apart (so that one could be stung tightly, the other loosely). Throats were short, wide, open, connecting with the head in the center, or way up on the sides. A racket was marketed with strings that went diagonally instead of vertically and horizontally.

One man's imagination yielded too much for the tennis world to swallow. In 1977 Michael Fishbach, a journeyman pro with modest credentials, arrived at the U.S. Open with a Head Pro Aluminum Model racket—sliver with a blue throat—that was conventional enough, except that its string job incorporated double loops, plastic inserts, rubber bands, glue, and who knows what else tied into the hitting surface. It reportedly was hand-strung personally by Michael himself at a very low tension. Michael, of course, dressed in similar fashion to his string job, with full beard (not closely trimmed), long hair, and a headband/bandana.

The loosely strung, handcrafted racket offered Fishbach an ability to impart enormous amounts of spin on the ball, hitting shots that would arrive on the other side of the net with such unpredictable trajectories that they were virtually impossible to return. The U.S. Open at Forest Hills was played on clay (the American green/gray version) and Fishbach set up camp at the back of the court and challenged all comers to deal with his "spaghetti" racket and its crazy new shots.

Fishbach and his "spaghetti" racket rolled through the qualifying rounds at Forest Hills and into a first-round encounter with Billy Martin. Martin had been the winningest junior player in the history of the game. His national championship victories in the eighteen-and-under division while still young enough to compete in the lower sixteen-and-unders made him famous throughout the tennis world. Early on he planned to spend one year at UCLA with Glen Bassett, just to pick up an NCAA trophy (1975), and then to move on to the pro tour. Everything went according to plan. As did his march up through the ATP computer rankings.

Billy is now the coach of the tennis team at UCLA and, in the Glen Bassett tradition, teaches his players that winning is a function of preparation. There was no way to prepare effectively for a U.S. Open match with Michael Fishbach. Fishbach made it look easy and went on to his second-round appointment with former champion Stan Smith.

To that point Fishbach was merely an amusing oddity, maybe a sidebar or casual note in the last paragraph of a news story. But when he felled the great Stan Smith in the second round, amusement turned to concern.

THE *WASHINGTON POST* DESCRIBED Fishbach as "an amply bearded, amusing, apple juice–slugging refugee from the satellite circuit." Fishbach played like a wildman, but he was a journeyman nonetheless. His racket was determined to be legal—they checked. Nevertheless, tinkering with the hierachy of our great sport was not something that would be smiled upon by the great powers in the USTA President's Box. It simply would not do that Michael Fishbach should invade the latter rounds of the U.S. Open—legal or not.

Thankfully, in the eyes of the USTA, Fishbach's run ended and all seemed quiet for awhile on the "spaghetti" front. Until . . .

In 1977 Guillermo Vilas posted one of the most phenomenal years in the sport's history. He won seventeen of thirty-three tournaments, posting a 145–14 record in match wins and tallied an open-era record winning streak of fifty matches, including the U.S. Open in a dramatic final over Jimmy Connors. A "spaghetti" racket brought the winning streak to an end. This time it wasn't Fishbach. But our own Ilie Nastase, wielding his own version of the "spaghetti" racket, who ended Vilas's fifty-match win streak. The unnatural spins, perverted strokes, and aberrant bounces that Ilie evoked drove Vilas to distraction. So distraught was he over his inability to deal with the uncharacteristic play that he chose to default in the second set of their match in Aix-en-Provence on October 3, 1977.

Ion Tiriac, who served as Vilas's coach, insisted (quite loudly by all accounts) that the racket be banned.

Now, remember, since the day that tennis was invented centuries ago and throughout the decades of modern competitive and professional tennis, no rule had ever been written to govern the size, shape, or weight of rackets to be used to play the game. Similarly no rule had ever been written that controlled the methods of their stringing. As USTA President Slew Hester once put it, "You can play with a tomato can on a broomstick if you think you can win with it."

AFTER CENTURIES OF PLAY with nary a moment's thought of regulation, Michael Fishbach single-handedly brought about a change in the most fundamental rule (or nonrule) of the sport—the equipment with which it should be played. The International Tennis Federation acted and they acted swiftly. In determining that they should protect against any development that would threaten the "nature of the sport," they voted to place limits on racket size and their stringing, but not on the composition of rackets. Nastase was left again to rely on his talent. Fishbach was relegated to the minor leagues, and for the first time ever there were now rules and restrictions defining the standard allowable designs for tennis rackets.

Concurrently, Howard Head saw an opening to revolutionize the sport—even within the newly imposed rules. Head was already a legend in snow skis. Innovative materials and design made his company one of the most successful in the world of winter sports. His biggest mark in the sports world, however, would not come until after he left the company that bore his name and introduced, under the banner of Prince, the oversized tennis racket.

While the Jack Kramer Autograph and most other standard rackets offered 85 square inches of hitting surface (and a sweet spot the size of a golf ball), the Prince oversized racket offered 110 square inches and a sweet spot that seemed bigger than the whole Kramer head. Players around the world laughed at first, calling the racket a flyswatter, a coal shovel, a snowshoe, and the frog prince, but Head had the last laugh. Company sales soared from $3 million in the racket's first year of production (1976) to $60 million when Head cashed in by selling Prince Manufacturing in 1982. He reportedly left with with a personal take of $37 million, since he owned 60 percent of Prince's stock).

PUT ASIDE FOR A MOMENT the impact of the oversized Prince racket on the professional game and think of the value that the racket offered to the average social hacker. Day after day in every city where tennis was played, huge numbers of weekend warriors and casual country clubbers ventured to their local pro shop to buy a better tennis game. Average players improved dramatically with the help of new technology. Using the racket turned "C" players into "B" players and turned "B" players into "A" players. Rank beginners who had difficulty making contact with the ball now found themselves able to actually play the sport because it was almost impossible to miss with the new large hitting area.

In 1978 the racket made its professional debut. At the ripe old age of sixteen, Pam Shriver reached the finals of the U.S. Open using the racket that was almost bigger than she was. Do you think any ladies at the country club bought the racket?

On the men's tour, Gene Mayer was still pretty much a journeyman who had yet to come into his own as a top ten player. When he became the first male pro to endorse the Prince racket, Gene became one of the most recognizable players in the game because he was featured prominently in the kick-off marketing campaign for the revolutionary new racket.

Most pros, however, openly scoffed at the new technology and deemed the Prince useless, at least for the true professional. Overwhelmingly, the touring ranks, who had grown up using traditional small-headed wooden rackets, felt that their rackets "had become extensions" of their arms. To be competitive against other pros, touch players felt they needed to play with a racket that felt comfortable to them, and no giant frying pan was going to offer that.

It's not that they didn't give it a try. A number of players made repeated attempts to use the racket. After all, Prince was offering sizable endorsement contracts for anyone who would make the switch. Most of the attempts, though, just brought frustration at the "lack of control" inherent in these large rackets. Besides, it was generally understood among my fellow professionals that the large head wasn't necessary because a true pro consistently hits the sweet spot anyway. We repeated this over and over to ourselves— with no small measure of arrogance. With our own large heads securely buried in the sand (or clay if you were European), we expected that the large rackets would be relegated to the masses while we pros would continue to insist on the more finely tuned traditional instruments.

Naturally we were wrong. It would take some time to prove our ignorance, but the end result was inevitable. By 1982 a full 25 percent of the players in the U.S. Open draw wielded Prince rackets. Countless more played with "midsized" frames sold by other manufacturers. And finally, to no one's surprise, a new generation of rookies eventually arrived who had never since early childhood played with an "antique wooden racket." It didn't help us veterans that these kids named Becker, Edberg, and Lendl were also bigger and stronger physically than the rest of us. The power game had arrived. Seriously.

Because the oversized racket was the invention of Howard Head alone, Prince held a patent on rackets of any size larger than the traditional eighty-five square inches. Out in the world of social tennis, the Prince racket took over the game much more quickly and completely than it did on the tour. The average club player now had no use for the old-style small racket—no matter who was being paid to endorse it. Other manufacturers of tennis rackets came to realize that they had no alternative but to enter the new market because volume sales records were being set year after year, and they were locked out of the party.

In order to get back in, the competing manufacturers were required to pay royalties to Prince on each oversized racket sold. This included midsized rackets, which became the default compromise of better players unwilling to admit they needed a little more hitting area. The companies paid and eventually the entire market was dominated almost exclusively by midsized or over-sized rackets.

Alternative materials, metals and fiberglass, were the next area of experimentation. Many different versions were tried and eventually graphite (or a graphite blend) became the norm.

Each year it seemed that the tide shifted ever more toward speed and power and a new wave of technologically improved rackets would hit the market. Indeed, the large-headed graphite Prince eventually came to be regarded as too weak in a world of wide-bodied rackets known as the Profile. These were introduced in 1988 and eventually Wilson's Hammer (a wide-bodied over-sized racket with all its weight in the head and a feather-light grip) took the concept even further.

How did this affect the professional sport? Gradually, of course. The first wave of impact was those players on the tour who had little difficulty making the early switch to bigger, stronger rackets. Gene Mayer comes to mind, as do his brother Sandy, Roscoe Tanner, and Paul McNamee. Players such as Lendl, Becker, Edberg, Wilander, and Noah certainly adopted the new "power game" rackets at an early age.

Generally speaking, veterans who tried to make the transition after several years on tour found it akin to relearning the sport. After virtually dominating the sport for years throughout the '70s, champions with names like Borg, Vilas, Gerulaitis, Solomon, Gottfried, Stockton, and Dibbs never enjoyed notable success after leaving the traditional wood rackets. Most of these champions certainly had plenty of years and (save for Borg) desire remaining.

It is often noted that previous generations showed greater career longevity and endurance than ours. Case in point, Laver and Rosewall successfully competed into their late thirties, with Rosewall even reaching the finals of Wimbledon and the U.S. Open in 1974 at the age of thirty-nine. I submit that a number of players of my era might have continued longer but for the arrival of "young guns" in the early and mid-'80s who were physically bigger and stronger and used more powerful equipment than our peers. In the early '80s the rest of us were eventually pressured by the manufacturers to abandon our wooden rackets—whether we liked it or not. The companies couldn't sell the small rackets to the public anymore and could no longer justify the manufacturing expenses, so they simply stopped making them.

An interesting side note on the subject of equipment is the emergence of equipment managers. Until 1981 I had never heard of such a thing, much less imagined what use they might be or what they might actually do. Wilson simply sent me rackets and strings. I would carry bags full of each to whatever tournament I might be playing. There I was provided stringing services and I experimented with tensions (stringers varied from week to week) until I found something that felt good. That would be my racket for the week. Warren Bosworth changed that.

The new fashion was to ensure that every racket in a player's bag would be absolutely identical. The manufacturers began to send a pro's rackets directly to Warren in Connecticut, where he and his staff would string, apply weight, shave grips, and so on to match each player's exact specifications. Each racket was then wrapped in an airtight plastic bag and shipped to the pro for use in tournaments.

Naturally some pros took this to the extreme. Bosworth's client, Ivan Lendl, became so obsessed with consistency that he would switch rackets at every ball change (nine or eleven games). His justification was that merely using a racket for that length of time would affect its weight, balance, and playing characteristics, and he didn't want to get caught changing to a frame that felt significantly different than the one he had just broken. Certainly the expense of strings and labor was no issue to Ivan, so he went with his theory.

Personally I felt that Ivan sometimes carried the concept to the extreme. One match stands out in my mind as an example. As Ivan played Boris Becker in the final of the Masters tournament in Madison Square Garden, I sat in Ivan's box with other friends and family. Late in the final set, Ivan finally broke Boris's serve for a 6–5 lead. You'd think at that point that maybe he was feeling pretty comfortable with his game—and his racket. It was time for a ball change, but Ivan was serving for the match in the final set! Imagine my shock as Ivan, during the changeover, actually pulled a fresh racket out of a cellophane bag with the intent of using it for the sole purpose of serving one game. He lost his serve. He lost the tiebreaker and the Masters title.

Rodney Harmon constantly made trips to his equipment bag during matches. He used one racket strung at seventy-one pounds when he was serving and would substitute with one strung at eighty pounds when he was receiving.

Borg, of course, was legendary for playing with rackets strung at eighty pounds, but Borg was also legendary for whacking the fuzz right off the ball and using enough topspin to make the ball hairless and airsick. It was no easy task finding a stringer who could get the right amount of tension without breaking the wood or the gut or both.

At the other end of the spectrum was John McEnroe, whose racket was strung at a relatively low fifty to fifty-two pounds of tension. McEnroe still went through more than a hundred sets of a gut a year. Bent underfoot, stomped to mush, cracked against Deco Turf, or torn apart with his bare hands, he probably went through a hundred or more racket frames a year as well.

When he switched to the midsized Dunlop graphite, McEnroe managed about two years of results that resembled his wooden racket success, but even his considerable talent (ball control, touch, and feel) was overrun by the power game that he could never play. The laws of physics just won't allow a flat shot to dive the way a topspin western forehand will. Hitting the ball harder would only result in the ball going deeper, and deeper, and deeper until it lands well beyond the baseline. The graphite blend did prove useful, in that it was more durable than wood under the stresses that only McEnroe can put on a frame. The space-age materials enabled it to fly like a rocket. I once saw Mac toss it from one baseline to the opposite fence—and that was with tendonitis in his tossing shoulder.

I'm told I was one of the last pros to win matches with a wooden racket and the last to reach the later rounds of Wimbledon and the U.S. Open with wood. I was extremely reluctant, to say the least, to part company with my Wilson Jack Kramer Autograph. It's hard to describe exactly how "as one" a player can feel with his racket, but that's how it was with me and my Kramer. It was the racket I grew up playing with, and it was the racket I won the NCAA championship with.

At the end of my first full year as a pro, I was lured away from this racket that was like a part of me. I was offered a lucrative contract to sign with Fila for my own autograph racket. Driven by ego and a rich payoff, I signed.

I was nowhere valuable enough at the time for Fila to reproduce the Jack Kramer Autograph just for me, so we had to find another plan. To their credit, Fila sincerely tried to develop a racket with the same playing characteristics as my frame. God knows, they sent me dozens of prototypes, all plain white with FILA painted on one side and BILL SCANLON on the other. The only distinguishing marks were the numbers: one through about forty-four. Whether it was me or the rackets, none of them felt right. It didn't help that I never had an opportunity to play with any of them for more than a few days between tournaments—I was just too stubborn to risk a real event with an unfamiliar frame.

The results were disastrous. The Fila Bill Scanlon Autograph Racket and Bill Scanlon, the professional player, could not peacefully coexist. The first half of 1978 was spent testing racket after racket, struggling to get results, and losing a lot of matches I felt I could have won. The last straw was at Wimbledon. Fila finally gave up on the effort to get me a racket I could use. But the contract stipulated that I was allowed to use the Kramer if they failed to do so, and I liked the money they were paying me. So we had a little problem.

As a temporary measure, Fila agreed to "Picasso" some Kramers for me to use at Wimbledon, or at least until we could find a way to terminate our agreement.

I got out of the contract as soon as I possibly could and returned to the Kramer. I never seriously considered using another wood racket, though the writing was on the wall when it came to graphite and midsized frames. On at least a couple of occasions, I tried to adjust to the updated, technically advanced rackets.

In early 1983, I was determined to make the switch to the Wilson midsized Ultra. Seriously. I spent three weeks in Dallas with Bob Mooty training exclusively with the new racket. I spent hours with Bill Stanley, the sports psychologist, mentally preparing for the transition, convincing myself that I could win with the Ultra. So many of the players were now using such rackets that many of us felt pressured to keep up. By the time I made the trip to the Gold Coast WCT Classic in Delray Beach, Florida, we all felt that I was finally ready to cut the cord and enter the new power generation. Wrong.

I arrived a couple of days early for the clay court event, played at Laver's Del Ray Resort, and had some good practice sessions to acclimate to the conditions. Rod Laver was there for the event and I had the opportunity of warming up with him prior to my first-round match. I was to play Marcos Hocevar, a Brazilian ranked thirty-seventh in the world. As I was hitting with Mr. Laver, I totally lost confidence in my ability to control the ball. This *thing* in my hand was so "technologically advanced" that it seemed to be able to think for itself and it certainly had no intention of doing anything I wanted it to. It didn't help matters at all when Mr. Laver, my absolute hero and my inspiration to become a professional player when I was a teenager, began commenting on my condition.

You'd think he'd have been more understanding, having gone through his own experience with a bad racket. Early in the '70s, he had signed a lucrative contract with Chemold to play with their aluminum tennis racket. In a single practice session, he bent four of them. This clearly was not a racket meant for Rod Laver. He returned to the Dunlop wood, figuring he had lost more in tournament earnings than he'd make in sponsorship with metal. I'm sure Rod knew what it was like, but instead of sympathy, I was getting his wry Aussie humor.

I went into a full-blown panic and at breakneck speed I returned to my hotel to fetch my trusty Kramers. Later that day, Kramer in hand, I made tennis history by defeating Hocevar, 6–2, 6–0, becoming the only player in the history of professional tennis ever to win a set without the loss of a single point—the perfect set, the "Golden Set."

GENERALLY SPEAKING, and especially after that match, I simply couldn't find the confidence to make the change, even though week after week I saw player after player gain advantage over me with their new equipment. Wilson asked me for the racket I had used in the "Golden Set" so that they could make copies, and I gladly obliged. The more Kramers I could get my hands on, the better. Not long after, Wilson surprised me with the "Golden Set" racket beautifully framed, but no more Kramers. To get the racket from me, they had concocted a story about making copies. I treasure their gift, but I sure would have liked a slew of Kramer clones to go along with it. As it was, I confiscated every Kramer racket left in stock. If anybody else wanted one, it was just too damn bad.

In 1984 Wilson finally ran out of Kramers for me, and I had no choice but to make a switch, opting for the Wilson Pro Staff.

By the end of the '80s, there were no wooden rackets left, and a generation of players who had cut their teeth on wooden rackets carrying names of homage like Jack Kramer and Stan Smith now held graphite or aluminum with names like the Terminator, the Exterminator, and the Thunderstick. The weapons of choice of the warriors on court had evolved. Just as tennis had evolved. And redefined the sport. Seriously.

5:

THE GAME GETS PHYSICAL

IF THE MARK OF THE '70s was to introduce tennis stars to the world as media darlings, then the '80s was a time when those stars shone as true athletes.

Connors, Borg, Nastase, Ashe, and McEnroe dominated the decade that started all the fanfare. They were so different in personality from their predecessors, but in one respect they were just the same: how they practiced their craft. Just like Laver, Rosewall, Roche, and Newcombe before them, this new crop of Grand Slam champions were talented shotmakers who were fast, agile, and long on endurance. They were artistic and graceful on the court but never notably big or strong. Points were won with strategy, setting up points so that a winner could be earned or an error forced.

Most tennis players, even world-class players who won tournaments like Forest Hills and Wimbledon and Roland Garros, practiced long hours but didn't dedicate themselves to training hard in the weight room. True power and brute force took a backseat to control and grace.

As junior players, most of our age group were advised by our coaches not to lift weights because the activity "used different muscles than tennis" and could actually hurt our tennis skills. Conventional wisdom prior to about 1980 was that tennis players should limit weight training to avoid "bulking up." Light weights and lots of repetitions were advised so that a player would remain flexible and fast. This was how it was done for generations and so it would continue. Until the '80s.

IN THE EARLY '80S, two Czechs made a significant impact on the thinking of tennis players and the evolution of the sport: Martina Navratilova and Ivan Lendl.

In her early years on tour, Martina was susceptible to the temptations of tour life. She readily admitted to being a junk food fanatic and she was usually a few pounds overweight by athletic standards. This is not to say that she was terribly out of shape. After all, she was still among the best tennis players in the world and she was making a living playing a sport. It's just that she might never have been mistaken for a triathlete.

Almost overnight, her attitudes toward physical training turned about-face and Martina became a virtual ambassador for physical dominance.

She delighted in telling the story of how her teacher in the third grade brought her to the front of the class to show the other kids what a bicep was. By changing her diet (her new bible was *Eat to Win* by Robert Haas) and diligently training in the weight room, she found an advantage that would put her at the top of the women's game for years.

Martina's training regimen will probably make you tired just reading it: She started with a thirty-minute off-court training workout in the gym created by physical therapist David Balsley.

1. Bike ten minutes, followed by sprints.
2. Lift weights to work on lower extremity body strength.

3. Begin arm drills. These are real killers, although they sound simple. Stand in place for one minute while making rapid arm motions as if running.

4. Next comes abdominal work: sit-ups, reverse sit-ups, and elevated sit-ups. Martina did at least a hundred sit-ups every day.

5. Then comes the stairs routine. Martina sprinted up fifteen stairs fifteen times.

6. Next are the upper extremities. On the Total Gym equipment, she used pulleys in reps of three sets of ten for her forehand, backhand, and overhead.

7. As her final gym exercise, Martina jumped in place on alternate legs for three sets of twenty. She then jumped in place on one leg for three sets of twenty.

Phew! Are you tired yet? 'Cause she's *nowhere* near done. Martina followed her gym workout by jogging a couple of miles to loosen up, then she'd take the court for on-court training drills. Her favorite? The *suicide* drill (and I'll just say that it comes by its name honestly). She followed drills by actually practicing her tennis. Motivated by her friend Nancy Lieberman, the well-known basketball star, Martina cross-trained on a different court, using basketball to improve her tennis skills.

The impact on her tennis results was dramatic. To this day, I don't think Martina is given enough credit for her absolute dominance of the sport. I have spoken of remarkable achievements by Borg and McEnroe and Lendl. Well . . .

Replacing her close friend Chris Evert at the top of the rankings, Martina would go on to win nine Wimbledon singles titles (six in a row). She mounted a winning streak of seven consecutive Grand Slam titles, and a ridiculous twenty Grand Slam doubles titles with partner Pam Shriver. They once ran a string of 109 straight wins. By the time she retired, Martina had won 165 singles titles and 167 doubles titles.

She continues to add to her remarkable record as I write. Her latest victories of note were the two Grand Slam titles in mixed doubles she added in 2003 at the age of forty-six. She is likely, even today, to be in better shape than many of her competitors.

Martina has always been quick to credit coaches and trainers, among them Mike Estep, Tim Gullikson, and Craig Kardon. Each had his own impact on Martina as he coached her at different stages of her career, but all had an easier time of doing their job because of Martina's intense desire and another common thread that has run throughout her remarkable long career: her discipline. Year after year, she not only maintained her regimen but actually continued to improve upon her skills and conditioning.

In the late '70s, Martina and I practiced together frequently at the Northwood Club when we both lived in Dallas. I once read a newspaper account that credited me with helping Martina with her game. Boy, did they have *that* backward. I can't begin to tell you what a positive influence she was on my career.

The time period was after I'd had some real difficulties (okay, call it a slump) and admittedly I was being less than professional in my training. Just spending time with Martina and observing the results of her routine were inspiring to me and caused me to step up the volume. I came to realize that you needed more than talent and shot practice. Strength and power played a big part in my resurgence, thanks to Martina.

Both Martina and Ivan Lendl subscribed to the *Eat to Win* diet of high complex carbohydrates and no sugar. When Robert Haas first put Navratilova on his diet, he declared that she would be "the first bionic tennis player." My own opinion is that she achieved that status mostly by strength training rather than skipping sugar in her diet. But she did claim that maintaining a healthy eating regimen enabled her to train harder in the gym.

John McEnroe, renowned for rarely practicing or watching what he ate, was known to occasionally poke fun at Ivan and Martina, saying that he was on the Häagen-Dazs diet. For the record Martina won more Wimbledon singles titles than all of Mac's Grand Slam singles titles combined, so maybe John should have given it some thought. For sure, sports nutrition had become an important aspect of athletic training.

I FIRST MET IVAN LENDL in 1980 during his rookie year when we played a first-round match in Denver. I won in straight sets and never really gave it much thought (I was the older, higher-ranked, seeded player) until a few months went by and Lendl shot up dramatically in the rankings. I also discovered something that was a little embarrassing. As I was pretty much unaware of his junior international successes, I mistook him for another Czech player prior to our match. This probably helped me, as I played our match with every expectation that I should prevail easily.

Later that spring in Milan, Lendl approached me about playing doubles together. Now with a clear view of how good he was, I gladly accepted. He wasn't so friendly later in the tournament, though, beating me in the quarterfinals. We did go on to play a number of tournaments together, both moving our doubles rankings into the top twenty. It was during that time that I learned a whole new meaning for the term *high sitter*. Believe it or not, even at that time Ivan had a great sense of humor. Unfortunately, most of his jokes were at the expense of his opponents and the press. (Q: What separates you from your opponents? A: The net! *Bad-ump bump*.)

As his partner, I became more and more impressed with his talent. Like Martina, Ivan wasn't the most gracefully talented tennis player on the planet. No one was likely to mistake these two for Nastase and Goolagong. But Ivan shared Martina's discipline and drive to improve every aspect of his game.

One conversation indicates the importance Ivan placed on power and strength. We were playing in Tokyo in late 1980 at the Seiko Super Tennis event, staying at the Keio Plaza Hotel. In the quarterfinals I was to meet Bjorn Borg, the five-time reigning Wimbledon champion.

The year 1980 had been a good one for Ivan and he had worked his way up the computer into the top ten. Two weeks before Tokyo, he had managed to beat Borg for the first time. Naturally I hoped, as we rode together back to the hotel from Yoyogi Stadium, that Ivan might give me an idea or two to help me beat Borg the next day. His response was interesting.

"Billy, you just rally with him in the backcourt until you get a forehand you like, then you crash it hard, cross-court."

To my thinking, this made sense and I volunteered to finish the strategy:

"And then I can approach the net because his backhand is vulnerable?"

Ivan just looked at me funny and said, "No, he doesn't get the forehand back!" I did get the last laugh, though, as I managed to beat Borg in three sets the next day.

In thirty years of observing professional athletes, never have I seen an individual more willing to work, train, practice, accept new coaching, and learn and improve as Ivan Lendl. No matter what area of his game needed improving, Ivan would simply go about the work necessary to make it a strength. I've seen countless other players become defensive or get offended at the suggestion that they might have a weakness, but Ivan always seemed to view his faults as opportunities to improve.

The most dramatic example of this was his physical condition. Ivan's physical fitness training regimen was grueling: calisthenics, running, bicycling, and weight lifting. On a typical day at home between tournaments, he would spend an hour on a vertical climbing machine, practice for ninety minutes, ride a bike twenty to forty miles, practice two more hours, and after dinner lift weights.

When Pete Sampras first joined the tour, Ivan invited Pete to his home in Greenwich to work out with him. Lendl was playing in the Masters at night, but he got up at 6:30 A.M., dragged Pete's butt out of bed, and made him do aerobics. Then they hit the court for a "friendly" little practice session. After Lendl got done running Pete ragged on the court, he sent him out for a twenty-mile bike ride.

I could totally sympathize with Sampras. After I was injured in a freak water-skiing accident, I underwent two knee operations, which kept me off the tour for almost a year. Lendl took it upon himself to help me with my rehabilitation and comeback.

Ivan Lendl embodies the maxim that hard training, self-discipline, and control of the on-court game will lead to certain victory. With Ivan's arrival, tennis became a game of power players, thus ending the era of touch players. Lendl had made power and athleticism the rule and he wasn't shy about letting the world know the discipline he used to achieve it. In fact, he felt strongly that by advertising that very fact he instilled fear in the hearts of his competition. Truly, I know of many players who tried sincerely to copy his training methods—only to realize that they couldn't keep up.

Ivan and I have had many conversations over the years about his eagerness to flaunt his work ethic. In fact, I often disagreed with him to a certain degree. Certainly Ivan did reassert his dominance over the rest of us and gained immeasurable amounts of respect. I'm sure that many opponents were beaten prior to even taking the court against Ivan because they knew how hard he worked. And how hard they *didn't* work.

On the other hand, I felt his reputation served to hurt his popularity with the general public. The fans had to respect Ivan for his training habits, but they didn't have to like him. By implication Lendl seemed to be saying to the world: "I'm not naturally talented, but I worked my butt off and I'm number one. I'm living proof that you don't have to be born with it, so the reason you're not successful is because you're lazy."

John McEnroe's PR machine, on the other hand, reminded everyone that Mac *never* practiced hard or exercised, that John was a star because he was just born lucky, that he was blessed with everyone else's helping of natural talent. For sure, McEnroe never gave people the impression that they too could have been champions if only they'd worked harder.

It was no wonder to me that, for all the respect Lendl received, the bad rap on Ivan was that he was just so "machinelike."

DURING ONE OF OUR TRAINING WEEKS in Greenwich, Ivan noticed me struggling and offered this advice: "Bill, you will never be in the same physical condition as I am, so get used to it." I was insulted at the charge. Who wouldn't be? Then I started to protest. He then explained very rationally, "I started a few years before you, so I have a head start. And since I continue to train at the optimum level, I continue to progress at the fastest pace I'm capable of."

And then Ivan added: "If you try to train extra hard in order to catch up with me, you will only burn yourself out or get injured by overextending yourself. The best thing you can do is to maximize your training at the level you are capable of, then maintain that pace without slowing down."

As machinelike as this sounds, it was a simple truth that still is one of the most important lessons any professional can learn. Since retiring, I have tried to pass it along to some of the aspiring young guys in Los Angeles. I just hate to see talented young players with great potential fail to realize their dreams due to injuries that might be avoided with the proper training.

Of course by the mid-'80s all the tennis world was aware of the great advantage that physical strength played in winning. Not only Lendl and Navratilova, but Becker, Edberg, and several others were beginning to show those benefits. So, as you can imagine, it didn't end there.

As expected, there would be players who hoped they might gain the physical advantage a little easier, without all the rigorous training. There were lots of theories on how a player might do this, but at the end of the day I'm not aware of a single approach that produced significant results over any real period of time.

When he was trying to make his own comeback after seven months off the tour, John McEnroe was observed chomping away on something called a Fiber Energy Bar. These bars were not (at the time) the common dietary aid that they are now and a lot of people openly speculated about what "secret ingredient" might be in those bars. Some people claim they feel more energetic after eating them, but they never did much for me.

Mac moved on from those to some magical potion concocted by a mystical mentor/guru. Mr. Mentor/Guru—John's savior du jour—actually ran onto the court during a changeover in a match against Brad Gilbert, declaring an emergency, and practically poured the secret formula down Mac's throat. It didn't seem to work.

McEnroe went through three or four different mentor/guru types (we thought one was a hypnotist) over a two-year span, each with a magical formula guaranteed to succeed. I'm fairly certain, judging by Mac's on-court behavior and the subsequent results, that they didn't work either.

Mac desperately wanted back in the game, and a lot of people wondered just how desperate he was. That was the dark side of the trend from touch to power: how far players were willing to go to get that edge in the power game. Nothing seemed to work.

At the risk of sounding machinelike, it seems that John's lack of success at making a comeback was because Mac didn't *work*. Or at least he didn't work hard enough.

In the mid-'80s, there were rumors about players dusting their wristbands with cocaine, taking occasional snorts to perk them up on big points. The wristband rumor became something of an "urban legend" on the circuit; something so bizarre you knew was untrue, wondering at the same time how any sane mind could even imagine that something like that could help your tennis. But it was something you heard so often that you tended to wonder about it anyway. It seemed to have started when some rehab doctor gave an interview in which he claimed he was treating players who confessed to the practice. Personally I think the doc was just trying to get some free publicity.

There were also rumors about players popping amphetamines. Yannick Noah openly complained in the locker room and to the press after one match that he knew his opponent was on speed because his pupils were dilated. Guess who won. Yannick himself admitted in a controversial press interview in 1980 that he had smoked hashish, but never before a match.

Yannick Noah was one of the most physical players on the tour and he definitely looked the most athletic of all the players. Had he not chosen tennis, he might have played well in a variety of other sports. I know that he worked hard, but Yannick was a true Frenchman in that he also played just as hard. His work ethic never got in the way of his smoking, drinking, or partying. And on the heels of winning the French Open in 1983, he rose to a level of celebrity in France that had not been seen since the Three Musketeers. To this day Yannick is still a favorite in Paris and has become a legitimate rock star in France.

The press in the '80s was so desperate for a story, any story that would play in the national media, that they would accept almost anything if it was spoken about a celebrity athlete. Just to take them along for a ride, Noah once offered that he had sex in the locker room just before a match. He won. I'm sure that the press corps expected it to start a trend.

I can't say with absolute certainty, but I think it was Arthur Ashe who first publicly suggested in his syndicated column in the *Washington Post* that there should be drug testing in tennis. This was in early 1982 and he informally polled players for their opinion on the subject. Use of drugs socially was a major issue in the news and popular culture, so questions were always posed of athletes. The results of Arthur's informal poll were about fifty-fifty.

The MIPTC then established a relationship with Comp-Care (a company employed by other sports to deal with drug-related issues) to anonymously treat drug abuse, but not until the latter part of the '80s did drug testing begin on the men's tour. Beginning in 1986, players were to be tested at two of the five two-week-long tournaments on the schedule.

The tournaments would be selected at random from among the four Grand Slams and the Lipton Players' International. The testing was for recreational drugs only and not for those that would be considered "performance-enhancing." Remember, back then Viagra had not yet been invented.

There were also rumors about players using steroids. I'll go on the record right now and say I have no personal knowledge of any tennis player ever using steroids. I never used them, never saw them used, and no one made any guilt-ridden confessions to me. Having said that, I am personally aware of several guys who played football for the Dallas Cowboys during that time who made no secret about their use. But as for tennis, I heard lots of talk in locker rooms and players' lounges and restaurants about players who were suspected of using steroids, but none of it was ever backed up by hard facts.

The first name I ever heard linked with steroids was Slobodan ("Bobo") Zivojinovic. I think this was totally unfair because I personally never saw anything to suggest that he ever used them. I'm sure that some people just couldn't imagine that a guy could be six-foot-six with that build and still move like a real athlete. Apparently these people have never heard of basketball. Still, Zivojinovic was from eastern Europe, where drug use among the Communists is not totally unheard-of . . . uh, seriously.

Becker's name often popped up as well. This was also totally unsubstantiated and equally unfair. Again, how could a young kid be so tall, so strong, so fast, and so talented (not to mention rich, good-looking, and smart) unless he had been using some sort of drugs? Speculation about who did or didn't use steroids on the tennis tour just became regular locker room talk. I don't think anyone ever learned much from it, but there was plenty of talk.

John McEnroe's name was also bandied about in these discussions (of course—his name was bandied about in most discussions that had anything to do with tennis), so I wasn't surprised to hear his now estranged wife, Tatum O'Neal, allege that her former husband used steroids during his comeback bid. Her statements seemed to be shocking "news" to the press. To me, this is just another case of unfounded allegations that have never been proven. Have you ever seen John McEnroe's body? I rest my case.

Making a comeback is a difficult thing to accomplish: physically, mentally, and emotionally. The pressure is enormous. The expectations you place on yourself and that others place on you are staggering. I know from personal experience, having had the two knee operations that I mentioned earlier.

When I tried to come back I believe I actually got in better physical shape than I was before the operations. But it is very difficult to regain the competitive edge. Perhaps it is an issue of confidence—or the fact that other players don't seem to fear you the way they did before. Remember, the overall level of play was rising rapidly at the time. For all my hard work during my comeback attempt (and all the help I got from Bob Mooty, Bill Stanley, and Ivan Lendl), I eventually came to accept the fact that it was unrealistic to believe I could get back to my previous rankings at the age of thirty or older.

I can only begin to imagine what the pressure must be like to attempt a comeback if your name is John McEnroe. Being one of the world's most recognized athletes, everything McEnroe did was public knowledge and he lived every day under a microscope. Besides, anything John accomplished short of regaining the number-one ranking would have been a disappointment. It's not often that I have a lot of empathy for the guy, but that must have been one helluva climb.

In more recent years the drug accusations have continued, and there have been suspensions and fines levied by the ATP Tour. Petr Korda was suspended by the tour after testing positive for a prohibited substance, a charge he vigorously denied to no avail.

AUTHOR'S NOTE: I don't want to be too critical of our sport or any individual players on our tour during that time or since. While drugs are a serious issue and drug testing is necessary to ensure that players don't abuse prohibited substances, my sense is that any tennis players associated with the banned substances would seem to be exceptions in a mostly clean sport. In over fifteen years of regular testing, there have been precious few cases brought to bear.

Worldwide there are numerous sports, professional and otherwise, that are constantly besieged with allegations of abuse and real problems stemming from this serious issue. Tennis has been fortunate to be mostly exempt from these problems, and for that we are fortunate. Seriously.

6:

SUPPORT SYSTEMS

THERE MIGHT HAVE BEEN great coaches before Harry Hopman, but in the tennis world he comes to mind as the first larger-than-life teacher who impacted a generation of champions. Hopman was a fine player himself, but it was as coach and captain of the Australian Davis Cup team that he found his place as a legend in the sport. Over the years he guided championship teams from Hoad and Rosewall to Laver, Emerson, and Stolle to Newcombe and Roche and finally to John Alexander and Phil Dent.

Interestingly, Hopman never worked as personal coach to any individual player. He was employed by the LTAA (Lawn Tennis Association of Australia) and his responsibility was to Australia's Davis Cup team. But it was impossible for Harry to limit his interest to just those two or three stars who happened to be on the team. Australia had produced a crowd of great players and he loved to coach. It was just his nature to offer all he had to any young talent who sought his advice.

I first met the legend after he'd stopped touring and taken a position at the PWTA (Port Washington Tennis Academy) in Port Washington, New York. Hy Zausner owned the club and dreamed of creating a "school" where young tennis players would learn from the very best coaches. He paid dearly for the greatest coach of all time. It was at the PWTA that Hopman created the prototype for today's modern tennis academies. His method was to feed balls from a shopping cart to the student at the other end of the court. The student's job was to give every ounce of energy he had to chasing balls and executing shots. Hopman would settle for no less than Rod Laver himself had given, and the students knew it.

The club was proud host to top national junior events and was a training ground for exceptional talent. Eventually, another great champion, Tony Palafox, would join Hopman at Port Washington and add his personal touch. Vitas Gerulaitis and John McEnroe are both products of Mr. Zausner's vision and Harry Hopman's experience.

Mr. Hopman was a larger-than-life inspiration to the young players who were fortunate enough to pass through the academy for junior tournaments. The academy approach was new and we were all aware of Hopman's coaching success.

Most tennis professionals until that time period were encouraged primarily by parents who had a strong interest in the game or at least by an individual who nurtured the player's interest. Typical of this example is Arthur Ashe, who was raised in Richmond, Virginia, and mentored by Dr. Walter Robert Johnson, a local tennis teacher who identified Ashe's potential from an early age.

The most common pattern of development was that successful young players would rise through the junior ranks from climates that allowed year-round play, such as Florida and California. There was little organized training, though, and most of the top juniors were products of a teaching pro who took an interest or parents who loved the game. Even Southern California, a powerhouse of junior tennis in the '60s, produced players from a combination of several development schemes under the umbrella of the SCTA's Perry Jones. So strong was the competition in Southern Cal that top juniors would leave their hometowns to train there.

Jimmy Connors, Billy Martin, and Trey Waltke all migrated to Los Angeles to pursue their tennis dreams.

After a promising junior career, the next step in a player's development was most often to join a top college tennis program. Dick Gould's program at Stanford has been one of the best in the country for over thirty years, producing players such as Roscoe Tanner, Sandy Mayer, and John McEnroe. Ten NCAA champions have come out of Gould's programs. George Toley coached for twenty-six years at USC, turning out players like Stan Smith, Raul Ramirez, and Bob Lutz before turning the program over to Rick Leach. The tradition continues.

Glen Bassett made UCLA a tennis powerhouse. His credits include Arthur Ashe, Jimmy Connors, and Billy Martin, who took over the program on Bassett's retirement. Clarence Mabry developed a tradition of winning at my school, Trinity University in San Antonio, Texas. One of his earliest players was my long-time coach, Bob Mooty. In the early '60s Mabry's team counted four players ranked among the top twenty males in the United States. One of those, Chuck McKinley, would play *and win* Wimbledon after his junior year at Trinity. He returned to play his senior year on the Trinity team as defending Wimbledon champion. Future Trinity players such as Dick Stockton, Brian Gottfried, and myself had large shoes to fill.

It was a time period when these collegiate tennis programs were considered to be "finishing schools" for aspiring American tennis professionals.

This generally accepted curriculum gradually evolved into one called "Take the NCAA title and run." Jimmy Connors and Billy Martin made it clear from the start that they intended to spend no more than a year in college. They were right. Each jumped ship with NCAA titles after their freshman years at UCLA. I left Trinity after winning the NCAA's in my sophomore year and John McEnroe surprised everyone by attending college at all after reaching the semifinals of Wimbledon fresh out of high school.

He lasted a year, casually picking up the NCAA trophy on his way out the door.

After a few years, even that plan seemed bothersome to the true prodigy, who would skip college altogether (and maybe even high school) in lieu of attending what was essentially tennis boot camp.

In the late '70s, Hopman left Port Washington and started Hopman's International Tennis Academy at the Bardmoor Country Club in Largo, Florida. At approximately the same time, another similar academy was being created by another successful coach, Nick Bollettieri. The Nick Bollettieri Tennis Academy settled in Bradenton, Florida, just down the road from Hopman's. The academies were revolutionary and remarkably successful. Kids and adults alike would flock to the academies in hopes of improving their games under the tutelage of the great coaches.

In order to attract the world's top talent, each academy offered scholarships and hired staffs of teaching pros that would even travel to tournaments with the kids.

For years, wave after wave of top talent would come out of the academies. American and international parents would send their children to live at the academy, attend special schools to accommodate long hours on the court, and learn from the masters who had taught Gerulaitis, McEnroe, Laver, Rosewall, Arias, Krickstein, Agassi, Seles, and Kournikova. Interestingly, in spite of the successes of these academies, few entrepreneurs have attempted to copy the model. And even fewer have survived.

Another phenomenon occurred in the '70s that would change the face of life on the pro tour. Lennart Bergelin, a onetime Swedish Davis Cupper and three-time Wimbledon quarterfinalist, was hired by the Swedish Tennis Federation in 1970 to coach two dozen promising junior players. In time one of those prodigies stood out as an exceptional talent. His name was Bjorn Borg. When young Bjorn Borg turned pro, he traveled full time with his coach, Lennart Bergelin, in tow.

Bergelin arranged literally everything for Borg so that his concentration could be 100 percent on tennis. Bergelin fixed his travel schedule, his meal schedule, his practice schedule, and he even woke Borg up in the morning. He screened all Borg's phone calls so he wasn't constantly harassed by people looking for free tickets, reporters looking for a story, or groupies looking for some action.

One of Bergelin's more time-consuming responsibilities was taking care of Borg's tennis rackets. Bjorn traveled with sixty to eighty rackets at a time, all strung at an unbelievable eighty pounds tension and it wasn't uncommon for Bergelin to wake up in the middle of the night to the unmistakable *ping* of a string breaking. During the French Open in 1979, Borg broke strings on sixty rackets in two weeks. In São Paulo in 1975, he went through twenty-eight rackets in six days. Bergelin was indispensable to Borg.

Like so many aspects of Borg's life, his success found its imitation. Many of the pro players began to wear long hair, use headbands, wear skintight Fila shirts, and travel with coaches.

The self-proclaimed master of all coaches was Ion Tiriac. His first protégé was Ilie Nastase, his fellow Romanian tyrant. Inspired by his success with Nastase (and by Ilie's retirement from competitive play), Ion took on Guillermo Vilas. The relationship between Tiriac and Vilas was interesting, to say the least. An interesting blend of Mephistopholes, Svengali, and Machiavelli, Tiriac was an entire entourage in one person: adviser, manager, agent, promoter, tactician, and consummate entrepreneur. Under Tiriac's tutelage, Vilas went from journeyman to number one in the world.

Tiriac was the "total coach." Never before and never since has the game seen anyone like him. If on-court coaching had been legalized, tennis would have missed out on sheer artistry in Tiriac's infamous signals. Lord knows, he and his prodigies would have been lost if Tiriac had quit smoking. One of his most famous tricks was to switch his cigarette from hand to hand to indicate where he wanted his player to serve.

Ion even dictated what clothing Vilas would wear on the court. I once observed a painfully long demonstration of Tiriac's ability to make a point in Palm Springs, California. Vilas was under contract to wear Fila clothing and had received several boxes (yes, several) of outfits at the tournament personally delivered by the Fila representative. Unfortunately, not every single shirt matched Tiriac's exacting design specifications. One by one and very slowly Ion pulled each shirt from its box and detailed to the rep exactly why it was (or was not) acceptable, according to his expectations. As it turned out, quite a few of the shirts failed to make the grade, resulting in some very happy locker room attendants.

The partnership between the two stars was the subject of much speculation. Rumors went to each end of the spectrum, including one that had the two as a fifty-fifty partnership on every aspect of Vilas's career. That version was supported years later when Tiriac's next protégé, Boris Becker, broke onto the world scene.

My first awareness of Boris Becker occurred at Wimbledon in 1984. As the number-twelve seed, I had advanced through to the third round of the event and was scheduled to have a day off while two young players fought to earn a spot as my next opponent. When I checked the draw I realized that I had no real knowledge of either of them. I decided it might be arrogant (and foolish) to assume that since I was the favorite I should ignore that fact, so I arranged with Peter Dennis, my coach at that time, to go and "scout" who I would play next.

Since the match was scheduled for 2:00 P.M. and was to be the best of five sets, we agreed to show up forty-five minutes later to let them get a good start. Bad idea. When we arrived Boris Becker led his opponent, 6–0, 6–0, 4–1. We got to see all of two games and learn nothing at all except that Boris was already an excellent young player.

My match against Becker was scheduled for the next day on Court Two. This was not good news for me (the seeded player) because that court had for years been known as "the Graveyard," site of many Wimbledon upsets. It also wasn't comforting to see

Tiriac sitting in the front row for our match. Fortunately for me, Boris (he was sixteen!) was still learning from Ion, and I managed to gain a two sets to one advantage, mainly on the strength of my experience and confidence.

In the fourth set Boris rolled over on the grass court and injured his ankle. As we sat together on the side of the court applying ice to the injury, I must admit that I was relieved to have advanced without finishing the match. It would be three years before Becker would lose another match at Wimbledon.

As Becker made his move up the ATP computer rankings, we learned more about his relationship with Ion Tiriac—and Tiriac's relationship with Vilas. It came to light that Tiriac and Vilas were, in fact, fifty-fifty partners and one of their business ventures had been to "invest" in young Boris. According to the deal struck with Becker's parents, Tiriac would become the player's manager, coach, trainer, ad infinitum, and take complete control of the kid's career. In return, Becker would "share" the earnings from prize money, appearances, endorsement contracts, and whatever else came their way. It was Vilas who pointed out that he happened to be Tiriac's equal partner. And that meant that Guillermo was, in effect, Becker's co-manager.

It is simply impossible to pigeonhole Tiriac into any one category, to label him with any one title. Tiriac engendered huge success for his protégés. For Becker he garnered contracts that were possibly the richest in sports history. But there was also a huge piece of the pie sliced for himself. By the late '80s, Tiriac's empire, T-V Enterprises (Tiriac and Vilas), was worth an estimated $60 million.

When it came to on-court coaching, Tiriac was the master, but he wasn't alone. Vitas Gerulaitis's coach, Fred Stolle, might touch his nose or scratch his ear to tell Vitas to go to his backhand on an approach shot. Bob Brett, Owen Davidson, and Warren Jacques were all masters of the subtle gesture that only a player might recognize as instruction.

Naturally there was much discussion of legalized coaching on the court. A tempest in a teacup, if you ask me. To actually legalize coaching on-court would only ruin a lot of fun. It certainly wouldn't have any effect on what was actually taking place. If your coach isn't smart enough to find a way to let you know what he thinks while sitting on the sidelines, you probably need a new coach.

I actually traveled with a new coach for a few weeks who disappointed me with his observation skills. A match I played against McEnroe in Madrid was the last straw. I was having one of those good days, serving every single ball to John's backhand on a fast indoor court. I was broken in the first game, but after a short time John figured out my tactics and began overthinking each return: literally standing there, knowing exactly where the ball was coming, and getting anxious about it.

The result was that he went crazy. There were games he couldn't even find the court with his backhand. It was the most extreme example of how well Bob Mooty's plan could work and to hear John agonizing about how that "asshole hits the same goddamn shot every f**king time" was priceless.

Unfortunately, I was never able to break John's serve on the fast court, even though I had set point in the second set. I lost the second set tiebreaker and the match.

In the locker room after the match, I was consoled by my coach, who complimented me on the match and, particularly, my serving. He thought I'd done a good job of "mixing it up" and "keeping John off-balance." As much as I appreciated the consolation, I decided I needed a new coach.

One of my favorite match episodes involved a girlfriend of mine who became a "coach" quite unexpectedly one summer afternoon during a doubles match at Queen's Club in London. We'd only met recently and begun dating, so I enjoyed her being at my matches, but we'd never even talked about tennis up to that time. As the match began, it was obvious that our opponents were using hand signals to communicate whether the net-man would cross on their service points. My new girlfriend picked up on this and casually (and very discreetly) relayed the signals to me as she stood on the sidelines.

I think our opponents thought I was clairvoyant. I'm not sure if it was legal, but it was one of the most fun doubles matches I ever played.

One coach on the women's side managed to get around the no-coaching rule by using a radio transmission (speaker and earpiece) to communicate with his player in Sydney, Australia, until they were caught in the quarterfinals.

There were other factors to consider in the discussions of coaching and its impact on the sport. What about fairness of competition between players who could and could not afford personal coaches? And, of course, there is the issue of line calls and other disputes. Can you imagine Ion Tiriac in the face of umpire Ken Slye? (TRUE STORY: Ion Tiriac once actually dragged chair umpire Bertie Bowron around by the ear in the locker room because he was upset over a call.)

Pancho Segura, Jimmy Connors's sometime coach, weighed in on the opposite side of the argument early on. He called the rule barring coaching from the sidelines "... the stupidest thing in tennis."

He argued that coaching could make matches longer and better. He also pointed out that having a coach at the player's side could be used to keep a player in line. Pancho said, "If he starts acting up, you grab him by the neck and say, 'Look, you little. . . .' " (I don't know about that one; I just can't see anyone shaking Jimmy Connors by the scruff of the neck. . . .)

A natural outgrowth of the coaching trend begun by Bergelin and Tiriac was the professional touring coach. This seemed to evolve in the early '80s as players recognized the value of having a coach but were a little put off by the expense. Generally speaking, a coach would about double a player's weekly traveling expenses, before paying the coach's salary. Rather than employing a player's hometown coach, often players would share expenses and hire a communal coach, forming somewhat of a team. Bob Brett was one of the earliest tour coaches who utilized this design. He was, in fact, paid by a sponsor (Best Products of Richmond, Virginia) to travel with players who comprised the Best Products team. Over the years Bob was employed by numerous lesser-ranked players until gradually his stock grew and he was brought on full time by Boris Becker.

At first it was only the top players who could financially afford the luxury of a full-time coach along with traveling wives and sometimes children. Eventually, the benefits of a traveling coach became a necessity. Players realized that it provided more consistent training and added motivation, constancy of companionship, and thereby stable emotions through wins and losses. No longer were players subject to the "luck of the draw" with practice partners, dinner companions, and confidantes. It was yet another contribution to the evolution of the sport, raising the bar by enabling players to play at their best more often.

In 1978, at the age of eighteen, Ivan Lendl won the junior title at Wimbledon. By the time he'd played even a few months on the tour, it was obvious he was going to be a great player. On tour he was befriended by Wojtek Fibak.

Fibak and Lendl were opposite in every way. Wojtek was ambitious politically, while Lendl was focused solely on tennis. Wojtek was worldly and well connected by virtue of being Poland's only star athlete—Lendl's social life consisted of practice partners. Fibak collected art; Lendl had heard of art. Their games were opposite as well. Fibak played a delicate game that relied on touch and angles. His serve was once described as like "a leaf falling from a tree." Lendl hit everything hard and heavy.

Fibak decided to take Lendl under his wing. In Lendl, Fibak saw someone who wanted to conquer the world but didn't know how. Lendl recognized he could learn from someone so different from himself. Their relationship lasted five years, but both are insistent that Fibak was never Lendl's coach. Instead, Fibak influenced Lendl's renegotiations with Lee Fentress of ProServ when Ivan's management contract was up. He also introduced Ivan to many of the "dignitaries" who would materialize each week in cities around the world where there happened to be a Polish embassy.

The relationship was certainly not a one-way street. Over the years Fibak was known as somewhat of a wheeler-dealer, and there were occasions when Ivan provided an opportune bailout when some project of Wojtek's turned out to be mostly wheel and not too much deal.

Another phenomenon of the early '80s that would make its way to the forefront was the emergence of *sports psychology*. It was dubbed, to quote *Star Trek,* the final frontier. An early promoter of the practice was Dr. Jim Loehr from Colorado. A practicing psychologist, Dr. Loehr had an interest in mental toughness and peak performance. His studies led him to the tennis world and a wealth of athletes who were anxious to learn what he had to teach. He wasn't the only one and the chapter that follows is dedicated to the new phenomenon.

BY 1985 JOHN MCENROE certainly had more money than he knew what to do with. He also knew that the power game was passing him by, and he needed to improve certain parts of his tennis game. Personalitywise, John was never the ideal student who could travel under the tutelage of a mentor. Tony Palafox had coached him to the extent that anyone could, but Mac's idea of the team concept team was nonexistent. In fact, he never really had a "team" behind him until he had to perform what is the most difficult task for any athlete: making a comeback. When the time came, he too joined the ranks of those who could no longer go it alone.

First up was California pro Paul Cohen, who became McEnroe's traveling coach/trainer/nutritionist. Cohen had coached quite a number of top-ranked juniors over the years, but his selection by McEnroe was still somewhat out of the blue. Players of all

ranks watched curiously as they engaged in the traditional practices that had by then become commonplace on the tour. The
results, though, failed to show any great improvement.

Mac's "entourage" the next year was anything but traditional.
After John was blasted in the 1985 U.S. Open by Ivan Lendl, he
sought help from a variety of nonconventional sources, such as
chiropractors, therapists, and martial arts masters. If there ever
was any player who could have benefited from the services of a
sports psychologist (or a couple of sessions on a psychiatrist's
couch), certainly it would have been John McEnroe.

Everyone thought Mac had gone completely around the bend,
that he had finally succumbed to the enormous pressure of being
John McEnroe when he began to travel with what can best be
described as a curiosity: guru/mystic/mentor Seo Daeshik. It was
a pairing that bordered on the bizarre, John in his tennis whites
and Seo clad in white from head to toe as any self-respecting Yoda
would be.

Seo taught Mac that aerobics were healthy and soon John was
into yoga and yogurt—and breathing. During lengthy, pro-
tracted, vitriolic tantrums, John would actually pause for one of
those long "crouching tiger" breaths. Occasionally, McEnroe
would even take a breath before lapsing into a tirade, as if trying
to garner a measure of patience before explaining one more time
with emphasis just how right he was and how wrong everybody
else was.

I learned early the harsh reality that you simply cannot go it
alone. There are lots of reasons and the biggest is that the bar is
pretty high out there and to keep the pace takes a lot of training.
Some of the training just can't be done alone because it requires
someone to feed balls to you in just the right manner to simulate
match situations.

Another problem is motivation. Although most athletes are
self-motivated—hence their advanced skills—it is always easier
to go ahead and do the work if there is someone there to walk you
through it.

Of course the biggest reason to have a support system in place is because of the status it brings—that invaluable measure of one-upsmanship that is so critical to winning on the tennis tour. No self-respecting champion would dare show up alone to compete for such great stakes. Our generation perfected the art.

Anyone could have a coach. Borg did that, but his manager/agent stayed home at the office. In Cleveland, Ohio, no less. Not a lot of style in that, except that Borg commanded more off-court fees than any other player. Vilas countered impressively by carrying his coach and manager (all rolled into one: Ion Tiriac) on the road full time. Girlfriends were worth extra bonus points if they were famous (Vilas dated Princess Caroline, while Connors dated Marjorie Wallace, then *Playboy* centerfold Patti McGuire). McEnroe bucked the trend, often traveling without any paid companion, but he still scored points by carrying Peter Fleming around the world (and to the top of the doubles world) for years. And then there were all those sycophants who tagged along for free. Most players had at least a couple, but McEnroe collected these "friends" like so many baseball cards.

Without a doubt, nobody played the entourage game better than Jimmy Connors. Over time he even showed that it was not only important to have more hangers-on than anyone else, but that you should rotate them around and switch off every year or two. Some of the crew should have an actual reason for being there, like Pancho Segura, who contributed a lot to Jimmy's on-court thinking. Others should be a total mystery, like Lorne Kuehl, a nice enough guy who was Connors's one-man cheering section. Honestly, some professional boxers and rap stars could learn from Connors. I never figured out the need for having a bodyguard for a tennis player at a tennis tournament (or two if it was the U.S. Open), but Jimmy gave it a try for a few years. He hit the big time, though, when he arranged a laminated tournament pass for his chauffeur and sat him courtside (in August in New York City) in his black suit and tie.

One valid reason for traveling with a coach or friend is to provide some consistency from one week to the next. The sense of being alone is one difficult aspect of life on the tour. Because our Grand Prix Tour was scattered all over the globe, it was unlikely that the same group of players would be together from one week to the next. There were many reasons for choosing which tournaments I might play and the chances were slim that I'd find the same friends and practice partners following along. In 1982, for example, my weekly schedule went from Hilton Head, South Carolina, to Vienna to Paris to Baltimore to Munich to Chicago to London to Hartford, Connecticut.

Eight tournaments in eight weeks, with six transcontinental flights thrown in for good measure. I reached the finals in Hilton Head, Vienna, Paris, Chicago, and Hartford. I lost in the first round in Baltimore, Munich, and London. Needless to say, something was missing in the consistency department.

Of course, I don't mean to imply that life was miserable during all that travel. On this particular stretch I got to play golf in Hilton Head on a course facing the ocean and then tour Vienna, one of the most interesting cities in Europe. Paris was for years one of my favorite cities, so much so that I would spend free weeks there during my Europe trips. I found a hotel that I liked one block from the Champs Elysées and made it my home.

Back in the United States, I had a fun time in Baltimore with local friends before flying back to Munich. Unfortunately, that was a quick turnaround for me because I lost first round. My consolation was that I was friendly with the tournament organizers there, and they arranged for a couple of great nights on the town.

When I got back to Chicago, I hooked up with a few friends from my days at Trinity University, and we went out every night to a different restaurant or night club. All of my matches were played in the evening that week, so we never worried about getting in early. When I got to the finals, my girlfriend flew into town from Dallas with my brother and his wife. Despite my loss, we had a great time, even though I had to fly immediately to London.

Since we spent a month in London every summer for Wimbledon, the town almost became a second home for me. I had a lot of local friends, and of course, the night life in London is as good as anywhere in the world.

Although it was hard work traveling to different parts of the world week after week, it was also a lot of fun. Unfortunately, there's no way to avoid jet lag, and it is a fact of life that I played many matches on low energy simply because of the time changes. Fatigue can also make it difficult to practice and train as well as we should. I'm sure a lot of players would agree with me that some really bad losses were at least partly a result of poor preparation due to travel.

Traveling with a coach or friend can smooth out the "emotional roller coaster" that comes with winning and losing every week. There is some value to knowing who you're going to practice with each day and that someone will always be good company at dinnertime.

One interesting aspect of the professional tennis tour each week is that every player in the draw (save for the champion) gets reminded what it's like to lose. Sixty-four guys start on Monday and by Sunday night there are sixty-three losers. Sixty-three guys who have been told how bad they suck. Even if you made it farther than you expected for the week or had a good win, it was never fun to be handed your walking papers on Saturday afternoon.

Johan Kriek was one of the most talented guys on the tour. He reached the semifinals of the U.S. Open two years in a row. Kriek also won the Australian Open twice, back to back, beating my fellow Texan Steve Denton in both finals. But Johan was also one of the most unpredictable players on the tour—and very inconsistent. He took losing very badly. Once after a loss in Philadelphia at the United States Pro Indoor Championships (played in January), Johan left the court, skipped the locker room, skipped the press conference, and just kept walking. All the way back to the hotel—in his shorts and a sweaty shirt. It was about twenty degrees outside and snowing. We think he warmed up before walking the rest of the way to the airport.

Bob Mooty, the head tennis pro at the Northwood Club in Dallas, taught me my first tennis lesson at the age of ten and remained my most constant positive influence until my retirement in 1989. (He was still at Northwood, even then.) Over the years, we grew together and adopted a lot of new training techniques, some of which we invented and others we stole from Tiriac or Lendl or Bergelin.

Besides being a perfect training partner, there were times when Bob's calming influence helped me get over tough losses and long stretches of bad results. We traveled together to Wimbledon, the U.S. Open, and the Australian Open, but one of the best experiences we had together was the formation of the Dallas Youth Foundation, a nonprofit organization we created to offer free sports clinics for kids in the Dallas area. These were not just tennis clinics; there were also clinics in football, basketball, baseball, and soccer. Members of the Dallas Cowboys, Bobby Valentine and the Texas Rangers, and the Dallas Mavericks all donated their time to the clinics and made them lots of fun for the kids— and for one overgrown kid—me.

I was pleasantly surprised at how easy it was to organize a foundation that would benefit so many kids. The whole project was underwritten by one of my sponsors at the time, the 7-Eleven Corporation, and one of my best friends, its CEO Clark Matthews. We had done a lot of traveling together and when the idea came up to start the foundation, Clark just said, "Go for it." The highlight of the foundation was when we had twenty-three current or former NFL football stars assembled for two hundred kids on the football field at Texas Stadium.

I also teamed up with the Maureen Connolly Brinker Foundation and the Dallas Tennis Association to support a junior development program in Dallas called the Junior Excellence Program. Also contributing their time for that program were Dick Stockton, Chuck McKinley, and Dennis Ralston. As much as any other sport or business that I've seen, tennis players seem to have a natural instinct to give back. Most of the players I've known have participated in junior development programs locally or at the national level.

Dick Stockton went out of his way to help me when I was a junior player in Dallas. Dick had won the NCAA Championships for Trinity University in 1972 and decided to base himself in Dallas while he played the Grand Prix Tour. I was lucky enough to get to practice regularly with him. About this time my father arranged for me to graduate from high school a year early so that I could get a head start on my college tennis career. What we didn't count on was that none of the top tennis schools were ready for me. Dick Gould at Stanford, Glen Bassett at UCLA, and George Toley at USC all told me they had no room for me.

I visited Trinity and met with Bob McKinley, the head coach and Dick Stockton's former teammate. His reply was pretty much the same—he felt I could use another year of development before playing at the college level. That was when Stockton intervened. On hearing of the situation, he picked up the phone to call McKinley and convince him that I would be good for the Trinity team. I'm glad I didn't let him down.

The year 1983 was my best one ever as a pro, and not coincidentally, it was the first year I ever traveled with a "professional" coach. Warren Jacques was an Australian transplanted to Texas, but he'd kept all his old Aussie values. Work hard, then enjoy a cold Foster's at the end of the day. Jacques had been hired as a touring coach about a year earlier by Kevin Curren and Steve Denton, both alumni of the University of Texas under Dave Snyder. Warren had known me since I was a kid growing up in Dallas, and in 1983 they let me tag along informally. There was never a formal arrangement between us, but we were "his boys." Much in the manner of Harry Hopman, another Aussie legend, it was just part of Warren's nature to be helpful. I also think Warren recognized that it would help all of us to have "teammates" who were also doing well each week. We watched each other's matches, practiced together, and generally motivated each other to push ourselves a little beyond what we might have done alone.

On a talk show in Dallas early in 1984, the host chided me because I kept using the word *we* instead of *I* to describe my career and the results I had managed to achieve over the last couple of years. But *we* made more sense to me. I don't think *I* would have accurately described the collective efforts of myself, Bob Mooty, Warren Jacques, my parents, my brother John, Richard Peyton, and Bill Stanley.

In the '80s, tennis was no longer that great one-on-one battle, just you and me so bring it on. Rather, tennis in the '80s was the Era of the Entourage. Everyone was a *we*. No one could go it alone. Martina Navratilova never appreciated the word *entourage*, and while she rivaled Connors in the support department, she preferred to describe her support system instead as a *coterie*. It was, she explained painstakingly to the press, a group of individuals that came together with a common mission.

It worked. Coaches, managers, agents, trainers, hitting partners, fitness gurus, sports psychologists, racket stringers, dieticians, bodyguards, therapists, publicists, and general helpologists all worked as a team with the common aim of getting through several tough rounds of tournament tennis to eventually stand at center court holding a trophy. No film ever won an Oscar without many individuals contributing their particular talents to the greater good. Why should pro sports be any different?

If a player believed a witch doctor could help with his game, a witch doctor would be part of his entourage. Success in tennis depended not only on skill or luck or physical conditioning, but on confidence and emotional equilibrium.

Tennis, that most isolationist of games, had become a team sport after all—or maybe group therapy. Dr. Phil, another Dallasite, would be proud.

7:

SHOW ME THE MONEY!

BY 1962 ARNOLD PALMER had established himself as golf's top drawing card. Followed everywhere he went by the legendary "Arnie's Army," Palmer commanded top dollar and drew crowds like no player had done since Bobby Jones in the late '20s. It was at that time that he asked his friend Mark McCormack, an attorney and fellow competitive golfer, to represent his interests in an endorsement contract negotiation with Wilson Sporting Goods. From that simple request grew the world's largest sports marketing firm, International Management Group (IMG).

By the mid-'80s IMG had grown to employ thousands, maintain offices on every continent, and represent athletes, entertainers, writers, politicians, and even the Pope. Likewise the company, and many others like it, would grow into event production firms that would represent every conceivable type of spectator event for sponsorship, management, and organization. It didn't end there. As spectator interest grew in their various fields of involvement, the firms would work to maximize the television rights opportunities in every market in the world and even create new events designed specifically for the medium. And they would encourage the creation of new product lines to be merchandised, taking advantage of brand identities like Wimbledon and the Vatican.

But it all began with client representation. When McCormack first began to handle Arnold Palmer's business matters, the golfer was earning about $60,000 a year. Within two years, McCormack had pushed Palmer's earnings to $500,000 by merchandising and marketing Palmer's name and image to Corporate America. The relationships have been brilliantly successful and very effective at marketing the companies' product lines, so much so that for most of the last two decades Arnold Palmer has dominated the world of endorsement contracts and other extracurricular earnings. This is remarkable, considering the fact that Palmer was well past his prime, or even the ability to be competitive, for most of that time.

Mark McCormack's greatest contribution is to have demonstrated to the world that people (specifically, customers) enjoy being associated with dynamic champions and will pay handsomely for the privilege of doing so.

On September 10, 1962, the same year that Mark McCormack and Arnold Palmer were forming IMG, Rod Laver won the United States National Championships at the West Side Tennis Club in Forest Hills, New York, to complete the fourth leg of tennis's Grand Slam. For his victory, the USLTA (United States Lawn Tennis Association) gave Mr. Laver a trophy, just as he had received from the LTAA (Lawn Tennis Association of Australia) for winning the Australian Open, the FFT (Federation François de Tennis) for winning the French Open, and the LTA (Lawn Tennis Association) for winning Wimbledon. The world's top tennis player did the logical thing. He turned professional so that he could compete for prize money and, hopefully, generate income from associating himself with sporting goods companies as Palmer and hosts of other professional athletes had done. This prompted his immediate ban from the Australian, the French, Wimbledon, and the United States National Championships, as they were designated "amateur" events and did not accommodate professionals.

To launch his professional career, Laver joined the foundling National Tennis League headed by promoter George MacCall. McCall had been the captain of the United States Davis Cup team from 1965 to 1967 before turning to the business side of the sport. Kenny Rosewall, Andres Gimeno, Pancho Gonzalez, Fred Stolle, and Roy Emerson rounded out the traveling troupe of tennis barnstormers.

Down in Texas around that same time, another larger-than-life force was turning its attention to the tennis world. Lamar Hunt, son of H. L. Hunt, the legendary oil wildcatter, imagined a traveling band of tennis professionals that would entertain fans around the world. Hunt was no small thinker and he was certainly no stranger to the sports world, as he was the owner of the Kansas City Chiefs and founder of the AFL (American Football League). It was largely due to Hunt that the NFL and the AFL joined forces, resulting in the world's largest annual television event: the Super Bowl.

HUNT'S RIVAL TOUR initially signed John Newcombe, Cliff Drysdale, Nicki Pilic, Tony Roche, Roger Taylor, Butch Buchholz, Pierre Barthes, and Dennis Ralston and called the group the "Handsome Eight" (or, as they termed themselves, the "Handsome Seven and Tony Roche"). So popular was Hunt with the players (and so successful was his tour) that amateurs were soon defecting to the pro ranks in droves. Hunt's original troupe of eight became an elite thirty-two, and ultimately Hunt swallowed his competition by merging MacCall's National Tennis League into his own tour. The result was known as WCT (World Championship Tennis), though Hunt quite enjoyed the term "Handsome Eight" and determined to make that the name for the finalists in Hunt's season-ending championship tournament. In 1971 he established the WCT Finals, featuring the "Handsome

Eight," to be played in Dallas. To top it off, he offered the richest prize in all of tennis to its winner: an astounding $50,000.

Rod Laver attempted to "manage" his own professional career and business interests for a number of years. Things were definitely a lot better in the professional world than they had been on the amateur circuit, but he felt he might be selling himself short. Laver approached Mark McCormack about becoming a client in 1966. McCormack initially turned down Rod Laver's request because he felt there weren't enough opportunities to "sell" a tennis player to make it worth his while.

In 1968 the national associations that governed the major tennis championships fell to the pressure to admit professionals. Open tennis had arrived. In 1969, the first full year of "open" tennis, Rod Laver won all four legs of the Grand Slam again. It is without a doubt the most remarkable feat in the history of the sport, considering he had been banned from competing in the game's top events for seven years.

THIS TIME, in addition to his four trophies, Laver received $5,000 for the Australian Open; $7,000 for the French; $7,200 for Wimbledon; and $16,000 for the U.S. Open.

Mark McCormack did an about-face faster than you can say "big bucks," and Rod Laver became IMG's first tennis client.

Players realized that it was important to capitalize on professional opportunities with open tennis, and thus they needed representation. Arthur Ashe, Stan Smith, and a handful of other United States Davis Cup players came to be represented by former Davis Cup captain and lawyer Donald Dell. Dell's law firm, Dell, Craighill, Fentress, and Benton, would form ProServ (Professional Services, Inc.), a sports marketing firm that, until 1983, would compete head to head with IMG for the larger share of the sports marketing pie.

It was in 1983 that a third agency was spawned when Dell and three of his partners, Frank Craighill, Dean Smith, and Lee Fentress, had a big-time falling-out. They disagreed over—well, pretty much anything and everything. The result after months of negotiations was that Craighill, Fentress, and Smith would form their own company called Advantage International Management. In an interestingly presumptuous gambit, the lawyers arrogantly divided their client list among themselves and "informed" the players, like so many cattle, who their future representation would be. Most players knew little about business practices and simply went along where they were told.

While IMG's beginnings were in the golf world, Dell got a big early lead in tennis that was predicated on a paradigm shift in the organization of the sport: the creation of the ATP. The term *conflict of interest* had never really been associated with tennis. Yet. However, this concept seems to have become a perfectly acceptable course by the early '70s, as Donald Dell and ProServ simultaneously represented individual players, the players' union, the ATP, and came to eventually own or manage a significant number of the Grand Prix events on the tour, as well as those nonsanctioned tournaments and exhibitions known as *special events*. The firm also represented a number of corporations, whereby for a fee they would advise on which events and for which players the corporations should spend sponsorship dollars.

In a given week, ProServ might own a tournament that was contractually a part of the Grand Prix Tour, enlist ProServ client players to compete in the event, own the television broadcast of the event, arrange for ProServ client players to endorse the products of ProServ client corporations, and, for good measure, Donald Dell personally would do the TV color commentary alongside another ProServ client.

When it came to tournament issues such as prize money and guarantees, the ATP players' representatives negotiated directly against tournament promoters of the Grand Prix Tour. Donald Dell and Jack Kramer were the founding leadership of the ATP, yet ProServ was among the most prolific owners of Grand Prix events.

Not to be outdone, IMG built a similar model, complete with their own TV production company, TWI (Trans World International), and an equally long list of events in Europe, Asia, and Australia.

As lucrative as its core business of client representation was, IMG was looking at the bigger picture and eventually devoted more of its resources to event management. As Mark McCormack adeptly pointed out, "Bjorn Borg can break a leg; Wimbledon cannot."

IMG had television and promotional contracts with three of the four Grand Slam tournaments. (Only at the French Open did IMG not have a significant financial interest and even there it held a commercial consultant role.) These major events are likely to be the biggest of all beneficiaries of Mark McCormack's creative mind. To visit Wimbledon or the U.S. Open today is to attend a major sports marketing convention. Virtually every major business interest/corporation in the world, from Donald Trump to Mercedes-Benz to IBM, recognizes the need to have a presence at these showcase events. Corporate hospitality VIP suites sell for hundreds of thousands of dollars and provide a venue for executives to entertain priority clients and customers. Sometimes they even watch tennis.

Mark McCormack and IMG pioneered the practice of providing tents, marquees, boxes, and any other perquisite imaginable to these major corporations. For a price. And IMG gets a cut out of every pound, franc, and dollar spent.

Ultimately, when the players seceded from the MIPTC's Grand Prix Tour and formed their own, proprietary ATP Tour, it was IMG the players turned to for marketing expertise. For a minimum guarantee of $56 million over its first three years, IMG became the exclusive agent for the ATP's sponsorship rights, television sales, and the promoter of the ATP World Championships. In real terms, that means the ATP was guaranteed a minimum of $56 million from sources generated by IMG. If IMG failed to deliver, they would be forced to make good on the contract out of their own pockets.

This was not uncharted waters for IMG. Both IMG and Pro-Serv had made a practice of *guaranteeing* a level of merchandising income to top stars. While it sounds risky for IMG at first blush, a longer look reveals that if Andre Agassi enters into an agreement with IMG with a *guaranteed* level of income from all sources, that agreement also obligates Agassi to agree to show up for *income opportunities* presented by IMG. If those *income opportunities* happen to be exhibition matches or special events owned by IMG (where IMG owns the gate, the sponsorship packages, and the TV rights), well . . .

IN 1987 IMG moved another step closer to dominating the tennis world by acquiring Nick Bollettieri's Tennis Academy. By participating in the development of young stars, the IMG representatives had the inside track on building those all-important relationships that will pay dividends in the future.

As the professional game evolved and more creative minds developed endless marketing opportunities, IMG and ProServ represented a majority of professional tennis players, but their tentacles extended into every aspect of the game. Without question, they were the main power brokers and gradually they became the most prolific tournament directors on the Grand Prix Tour. They managed the tournaments and marketed them. They shopped for sponsors, sold the TV rights, and provided the players. The influence of the megaagents was virtually inescapable.

Fees? Of course! Players paid ProServ a percentage of the prize money earned at the event and a percentage of their endorsement contracts with the corporations; the corporations paid ProServ a percentage of the sponsorship contract with the event and a percentage of the endorsement contract with the players. The event paid a management fee to ProServ to arrange players and sponsors for the event, the TV production company paid ProServ—well, you get the picture.

The standard representation fee for ProServ and IMG was 25

percent. Mack McCormack once said, "If I were to get the twenty-fifth leading tennis player in the world, or the fiftieth . . . a million a year contract, *and there's no way he can get that million without me*, then ninety percent might have been a fair price."

Total prize money in 1968, the first year of open tennis, was approximately $350,000. For winning Wimbledon that year, Rod Laver received about $5,000. In 1971 he became the first player to hit the $1 million mark in career earnings.

By 1987 worldwide tournament purses were about $35 million. The U.S. Open paid $250,000 to the men's and women's singles champion. Donald Dell's estimated earnings that year were $25 million. ProServ offices could be found in all the world's major capitals. Mark McCormack was a millionaire many times over. His empire, IMG, had fifteen offices worldwide pulling in revenues in the hundreds of millions.

When I won my first professional tournament, I split a $2,000 doubles prize. My first singles title at Maui in 1978 came with a $20,000 payday. By the time I retired in 1989, more than $50 million in prize money was available throughout the season. And that doesn't factor for one single endorsement contract dollar, or one franc paid for an exhibition appearance, or one yen delivered under the table to appear in a Grand Prix event in Tokyo.

Big-time money had infiltrated big-time tennis and players became the marketable commodity, subject to the laws of supply and demand. McEnroe, Connors, Borg, Lendl, Gerulaitis, Vilas— they had marketable images and marketable names. Fans would pay to watch them play. Promoters invested in exhibitions and special events where they could guarantee matchups between bankable stars, and tournaments on the pro schedule were in competition to get box-office draws as well.

In 1980 I found myself caught in a tug-of-war. It was the understandable result of the conflicting interests of players, promoters, and agents, and it all started when I was playing the Benson and Hedges Wembley in London.

After losing the doubles final with Eliot Teltscher to John

McEnroe and Peter Fleming, I was scheduled to fly to the next tournament in Bologna, Italy. Sunday night, however, I received a call at midnight from the office of Donald Dell. I was represented by ProServ at the time and they (ProServ) were promoting a rich tournament in exotic Dubai. The firm had "arranged for me to be accepted in the desert event," even though I was already scheduled to play the Grand Prix event in Bologna. In fact, I was a last-minute replacement for an injured player who had to withdraw. ProServ's advice to me was that I skip Bologna and make the trip to Dubai. A plane was set to leave Monday morning at 9:00 A.M. from Heathrow Airport.

I asked about the consequences of dropping out of the Grand Prix event in Bologna. I was thinking very rationally at midnight and worried about being fined or suspended by the MIPTC. The response was that first-round losers in Dubai were set to receive $25,000 and that any fine I incurred might easily be absorbed by the fat paycheck. And then there was the possibility of winning even more in Dubai. I took the flight.

It is an eight-hour flight from London to Dubai, but a long flight can be very entertaining when the plane is full of "rich" tennis pros on their way to some meaningless treasure hunt in the desert. About halfway through the flight, Ilie Nastase took over the service duties from the flight attendant and delivered meals to all the passengers.

WHEN WE FINALLY ARRIVED at the hotel, sometime after midnight, I was presented with an "urgent" message from Pro-Serv's Washington, D.C., office.

I called immediately, only to find out that the consequences of my skipping Bologna to play Dubai now would be more than a couple of hundred dollars. Bologna tournament officials had made very clear (with harsh threats) just what would happen if I didn't get my butt to Bologna in time for my first-round match. They refused to accept my withdrawal and they meant to make an example of me before the Men's International Professional Tennis Council (Pro Council). Withdrawing from a Grand Prix event to play an exhibition was an offense punishable by a fine of $10,000—and a year's suspension from the tour.

I reluctantly, but very wisely, boarded the first available flight out of Dubai: leaving at a 7:30 A.M. and arriving in Rome seven hours later. I was met at the Rome airport and driven at breakneck speed—three and a half hours at 100 miles an hour from Rome to Bologna, arriving with about an hour to spare for my 6:00 P.M. match. I lost (surprise) to Pavel Slozil, 7–6, 6–3.

Exhausted, I slept for fourteen hours that night and discovered the next day that the Italians were still not altogether happy with me. So I decided to go someplace where I was more popular. I found myself back in London the next afternoon.

In twenty hours I had traveled six thousand miles round-trip from London to Dubai to Rome to Bologna to London. I had earned a staggering $450 for losing in the first round in Bologna and lost out on a minimum $25,000 purse in Dubai. Mr. Dell's little conflict of interest hadn't been in my best interest at all, but I imagine he made out just fine on the deal.

What is it they say is the root of all evil? Money. Legitimate prize money offered by legitimate tournaments couldn't begin to compare with the *Swiss bank account* type of practices that were going on as a side industry.

Ordinary players made their living, of course, from tournament winnings, but the higher-ranked a player was, the more his income was derived from other sources. Relatively high-ranked players could add 50 percent to their earnings outside of match winnings; bona fide stars were able to tack on truly staggering amounts of money. More than any other sport, tennis was endorsement-crazy and the fees paid for exhibition one-night stands and special events were constant streams of outside income.

At the height of his career, for example, Bjorn Borg was the world's highest-paid athlete. He raked in an estimated $10 mil-

lion a year (remember, this was in the '70s—eventually, that fig-
ure would pale in comparison to Agassi's market potential).
Meanwhile, Mark McCormack laughed all the way to the bank.
Borg's tournament earnings, which alone made him a millionaire,
were just a tiny slice of the pie. His "official" tournament earnings in 1979 were $1,008,742. For endorsing the Donnay racket,
Borg reportedly made $600,000 a year; $500,00 for wearing Fila
clothes; $300,000 for wearing Diadora shoes; and $200,000 for
serving as "touring pro" for Caesars Palace in Las Vegas. Throw in
some not-insubstantial earnings for representing another fifty or
so products and services worldwide. Last, and certainly not least,
let's not forget the $500,00 a year Borg could command just for
playing exhibitions.

The amounts involved in Ilie Nastase's contract with Adidas
were comparable, mostly thanks to Nasty's far-reaching fame and
notoriety, and he didn't even use the racket he endorsed. In 1976
he became the first European to exceed $1 million in "official"
career earnings. (He was suspended a lot, but that gave him extra
time to play exhibitions and bring in a little outside loot.)

Jimmy Connors had his own line of tennis clothes, his own
line of shoes, a fat racket contract with Wilson, and his own tournament promotion company. Donald Dell eventually took charge
of Jimmy's merchandising efforts and matched his image with
such corporate needs as McDonald's and Paine Webber. Naturally
Jimmy also had innumerable bookings for exhibitions commanding six figures. Want to know his "official" earnings in 1977?
Only $428,919, a paltry sum by today's standards.

Ivan Lendl's deal with Adidas for a distinctive line of argyle-
patterned tennis clothes was said to guarantee him $2 million in
the early '80s. By the late '80s, his exhibition schedule included
matches at upwards of $50,000 a pop. In 1980, his first full year
as a pro, Lendl's "official" earnings were $583,906.

When Guillermo Vilas jumped ship from Fila to Ellesse, a
reputed million-dollar contract was the persuader. His racket deal

with Slazenger was said to net him $200,000. In 1977 Mr. Vilas topped the chart in "official" earnings at $766,065.

When John McEnroe's three-year contract with Wilson ended in December 1980, racket representatives were lined up with offers. He signed in the spring of 1981 with Dunlop, agreeing to use their Maxply Fort model for a reported $3 million for five years. (The deal paid off in spades for Dunlop. In the five months following his 1981 Wimbledon victory, McEnroe's Dunlop Maxply sales rocketed an astronomical 240 percent.) That adds up to $600,000 annually for using Dunlop rackets, plus another six-figure deal for wearing Nike shoes, and close to $500,000 for donning Sergio Tacchini clothes, plus McEnroe could easily command $75,000 an appearance for exhibitions. Mac's "official" prize money take in 1978, his first year as a pro, was $460,285. New racket in hand, his "official" earnings were $991,000.

Again, this was back in the late '70s and early '80s when the minimum wage was about $3.00 an hour and the median household income in the United States was around $20,000.

I ended 1977, my first full year as a pro, with "official" tournament earnings of $96,330. I signed my first contract with Fila for a *total package*: clothes and a racket. The contract was set up with a bonus structure. The higher I was ranked, the more I'd be paid. Unfortunately, I never delivered results sufficient to warrant any bonuses.

My ranking during my struggles dropped from 32 to 112 and my official earnings dropped to $47,908; a fairly small sum in tennis, but still in the middle-class range in society at large. The three-year contract turned into a one-year contract with a cash buyout at the end of the year. By 1983 I had worked my way back to ninth in the world with "official" earnings at almost $300,000 for the year. I'm glad to say that my appearance fees and endorsement earnings rebounded with my ranking. It was still small change, though, compared to the real stars.

Lendl's "official" earnings that same year were $1,747,128;

McEnroe's were $1,206,844; and Vilas raked in $677,035—"official" earnings from Grand Prix or WCT tournaments.

Every pro used rackets, shoes, and clothes with visible brands. Virtually every sleeve held patches promoting some product or another. Every player did not reap financial rewards or play in nonsanctioned tournaments for extra payola, but the "Show me the money" attitude that prevailed in tennis posed a major threat to the game when top players spurned regular tournaments for *special events*.

From one-night head to head superstar events to four-, eight-, sixteen-, or thirty-two-player contests billed as *challenges* or *shootouts*, there were eventually just as many *special events* as sanctioned Grand Prix tournaments. A player could make as much if not more in a single night (even if he lost) as he could slugging his way through a tough two-week tournament and claiming the trophy.

One of the most interesting events to emerge in the '80s was the Huggy Bears event held the week before the U.S. Open in Southampton, New York. Brothers Teddy and Tony Forstmann, legends in the financial world, host the world's premier Pro-Am event offering their very privileged guests and clients (some who would have trouble winning the B or C divisions of their club championships) the opportunity to compete with the world's greatest professionals. Prize money is through the roof—the winners taking home well over six figures. I enjoyed the Huggy Bears so much that I founded a West Coast (Beverly Hills) version of the event with my good friend Geoff Palmer.

For a touring professional, competing in special events is also a lot less stress and much more fun than official tournaments—not to mention all the ego gratification.

Just for fun, picture John McEnroe emerging spotlit through a mist clad in a cape with "Eye of the Tiger" blasting in the background, the announcer reading his credits, and the crowd cheering as if John was a rock star. It was great theater.

It was also pressure-free competition. The promoter, naturally, wanted an exciting match, the longer the better. In order to accommodate the promoter (and make sure they got invited back next year), the players might occasionally "orchestrate" the points, if not the outcome of the match. A typical scenario was to play the first set normally, and then "arrange" for the loser of the first to win the second. The players were then free to play it straight again in the third. I never heard anyone complain.

STILL, WHETHER THESE SHOWS were real or staged isn't what threatened the fiber of tennis—the real problem they created was that sanctioned tournaments found themselves having to compete to hire players. The hot-button issue plaguing tennis became *guarantees*. To ensure a top name player's appearance as a gate attraction, a tournament would have to pay a guarantee to that player above and beyond what official prize money was offered. In other words—appearance money.

It was not a new issue. Under the table payments were a throwback to the good old amateur days when some stars of the game received secret payments. I wasn't there, but the story goes that Suzanne Lenglen even received appearance fees to play Wimbledon in the '20s.

The practice extended into the '70s in matches billed as "winner-take-all." These matches were billed as heavyweight bouts between championship contenders. In reality, they were exhibition matches with substantial guarantees for both players. Eventually, the "wink and a nod" secret dealings were exposed to the public. Not only was this an issue of fairness in the sport, the Feds actually got involved with a couple of events when the FCC ruled that a TV network had "deceived the public" by billing the so-called *Heavyweight Championship of Tennis* as "winner-take-all" events. Connors was a regular participant in these matches and was routinely guaranteed approximately the full purse, win or lose.

In the early '80s, some players could easily demand big bucks up front above and beyond any prize money they might win. Tournament directors had to make the tough call. Without some top star, a tournament was deemed to be second-class, and just maybe unable to draw big crowds and sponsorship dollars. Essentially, tournaments would offer what amounted to a bribe of five or six figures to attract top players who would attract fans and sponsors.

The practice of paying guarantees was particularly endemic in Europe and even a Grand Slam event, the Australian Open, was not immune for a short spell when few of the top players seemed anxious to make the trip down under. Harold Solomon referred to the practice as "a cancer within tennis . . . no different from the graft a politician might take."

"No player shall accept money or anything of value that is given, directly or indirectly, to influence or guarantee his appearance," so read the Grand Prix rules governing such things. Tournaments and their sponsors were forbidden to "offer, give, or pay money or anything of value other than prize money to a player, directly or indirectly, to guarantee a player's appearance at the tournament."

The statute carried with it the right to demand all records "relating in any way to such alleged guarantees." Inducements in violation of the rules were subject to fines up to $20,000 and suspensions of up to three years.

Guarantees became the great schism of tennis in the '80s, pitting players against each other, but mere suspicion of the practice also created a witch-hunt environment. Who was guilty of paying them? Who was guilty of receiving them?

Rumors were flying almost daily about which players accepted how much to play where. Anywhere from ten to twenty-five players were said to be under investigation.

Johan Kriek openly crowed to other players when he received his first guarantee offer. It was a status symbol. He had joined tennis's elite. Somebody literally had to tell him to shut up before he brought a ton of trouble down on himself and everyone else.

The Stuttgart Outdoor 1981 tournament came under investigation by the Pro Council when a major red flag, lots of suspicion, and more than one eyebrow were raised. For the paltry top prize of $15,000, the final was played between Borg and Lendl. What would entice such high-caliber players to a relatively insignificant tournament? I'll give you one guess.

After the yearlong scrutiny by Marshall Happer III and the Pro Council, the tournament was found to have offered Mercedes automobiles as incentives to appear. The tournament was slapped with the maximum $20,000 fine, but no fine was imposed on a player. Tournament organizers refused to pay the fine. The Pro Council refused to sanction them, and the Stuttgart Outdoor was dropped from the circuit.

Happer was determined, though, to nail a player: a scapegoat, an object lesson, whatever; and thus someone was all but clamping a hand over Kriek's mouth.

Lendl came under investigation with suspicions of impropriety in a tournament in Milan. Guillermo Vilas was in deep trouble for his appearance in Rotterdam. The sharks were circling—and they smelled blood.

The Cuore Cup in Milan offered the largest purse of any non-Grand Slam tournament on the Grand Prix tour with $350,000 total prize winnings available to the thirty-two players in its draw. It had such an attractive purse that you'd expect the tournament to draw lots of players, even those in the upper crust. McEnroe and Connors entered, and no one looked askance at that. However, both Connors and McEnroe were forced to withdraw because of injury. This left the event with no real drawing cards and threatened its ability to recoup its payout at the ticket office.

McEnroe had been plagued by a sore shoulder most of the year. Connors's defection wasn't totally unexpected. He had dropped out of the tournament in Rotterdam at the last minute just a week before. The tournament was in disarray and backroom dealings were afoot. Lendl and Connors were both clients of Dell's ProServ. It also happened that Sergio Palmieri, the Milan tournament director, acted as ProServ's representative in Italy. (As I mentioned earlier, conflicts of interest were not uncommon at the time.)

At the last minute, it was announced that Ivan Lendl had been given late entry and the media hounds, smelling a story, began the hunt. The AP and UPI claimed that Lendl had agreed to enter the tournament after "intense financial haggling." UPI's version was that Lendl had been "hired" to play and quoted a tournament organizer as saying it was "the only way to save the event." As the tournament itself unfolded, Lendl reached the final after a close three-setter against Chip Hooper in the semifinals. In the final he defeated Kevin Curren, who had eliminated me in the other semifinal. As far as any of us knew (and as far as the general public knew), the tournament had been a success. What we didn't know was that Ivan's hide was hanging on the line.

The event had been held the last week of March. By May, Lendl had been served notice that he was under investigation by the Pro Council. By September, the tournament and the Pro Council were in a standoff. The tournament had refused to turn over their financial documents, wouldn't or couldn't give access to a suspicious bank account in Liechtenstein, or release the details of a contract between Lendl and a major sponsor of the Milan tournament, Achilli Motors. Pending the investigation the Pro Council still hadn't placed Milan on the 1984 schedule and were withholding sanction. Ultimately, the investigation ended in a stalemate. With both parties unable to budge past their respective positions, Lendl was exonerated and continued to play the Grand Prix Tour. The event in Milan, which had been dropped from the Grand Prix calendar, was quietly reinstated on the schedule.

The Pro Council didn't give up. Under the protection of lone wolf Ion Tiriac and not one of those powerbrokers IMG or Pro-Serv, Guillermo Vilas was an easier target. Within two months of losing a final in Rotterdam to Gene Mayer, a runner-up showing that netted him $25,000, Vilas was served with formal notice that he was being investigated for allegedly accepting a prohibited payment to play in the tournament. Vilas was a last-minute entry in the event after Eliot Teltscher and Jimmy Connors dropped out. The notice charged that either Vilas "or someone acting on Vilas' behalf" had received money as an enticement to appear in the event.

Interestingly, it was Marshall Happer himself who first contacted Ion Tiriac about Vilas's availability in light of Connors's and Teltscher's withdrawals. Tiriac managed to reach Vilas as he was waiting for a flight from Buenos Aries to Paris (without cell phones) and asked if Vilas would be interested in playing. Vilas agreed.

The gavel fell less than a month after Vilas was informed of the investigation. The tournament in Rotterdam happened to be a municipal event whose records were public information. Realizing that when their financial statement was filed with the city government all would be revealed, they turned themselves (and Vilas) in. Apparently, it was an open-and-shut case. Vilas was found guilty of accepting an illegal guarantee of $60,000, the payment supposedly having been given to Tiriac. Vilas was fined the maximum $20,000 and slapped with a career-crippling one-year suspension. The tournament was fined $10,000.

According to the rules, Vilas had thirty days to appeal, which he did, and he gained widespread support among the players, including the circulation of a petition to the Pro Council urging them to lift the suspension.

The petition said:

The undersigned wish to express our support for Guillermo Vilas and our belief that he has been unfairly fined and suspended by the MIPTC. Guillermo Vilas, always a gentleman on and off the tennis court, has been a strong supporter of professional tennis for the last ten years. He has entertained millions of people around the world, and he is primarily responsible for the rise in popularity of tennis in

South America. We ask the MIPTC to void the harsh sanctions imposed on Guillermo and to understand our concern over depriving, unjustly we believe, one of our colleagues of his right to earn his livelihood.

The petition was signed by players of widely diverse ranks, among them: John McEnroe, Ivan Lendl, Yannick Noah, Mats Wilander, Jose-Luis Clerc, Vitas Gerulaitis, Johan Kriek, Kevin Curren, Steven Denton, Wojtek Fibak, Brian Teacher, Henri LeConte, Henrik Sundstorm, Cassio Motta, Joao Soares, Ricardo Acuna, Florin Segarceanu, Peter Fleming, and Bill Scanlon. Notably, although he voiced public support for Vilas, Jimmy Connors didn't sign the petition.

In December Bill Talbert, Forest Hainline, and Vic Seixas heard testimony for Vilas's appeal. The director of the Sports Palace in Rotterdam, a Mr. Hoekwater, testified that Ion Tiriac had phoned on July 26, five weeks after the punishment was imposed on Vilas. He alleged that Tiriac offered the tournament director, Piet Bonthuis, $60,000 to change the books, erasing the payment to Vilas. Tiriac, the testimony further alleged, phoned again on July 28, and upped the ante, offering Bonthuis $300,000 to say that he had pocketed the guarantee.

Tiriac's testimony disputed this. Tiriac testified that he (Tiriac) "didn't receive any illegal money." He swore that a tournament official tried to extort money from him. In exchange for a huge payment from Tiriac, the man would issue a public statement that no payment had ever been given to Vilas. Tiriac refused.

Vilas testified, "I think it is illegal to receive such remuneration." He said he "trusted Tiriac," then he added, "I don't want to do anything . . . to damage my image . . . as an honest guy."

MIPTC counsel, Roy Reardon, gave what must have seemed a surreal response, "You realize . . . no one is suggesting you took any money."

After a month's wait during which the appeal's committee considered the evidence, Vilas learned his fate. The one-year suspension was thrown out, but he would have to pay the $20,000 fine. The three-member review board had ruled unanimously.

In the interim, *World Tennis* magazine published an article written by Steve Goldstein alleging that Connors accepted a guarantee to play the Grand Prix tournament in Las Vegas. Connors was said to have received the payment in cash in front of witnesses and to have signed a receipt for the money, which came from "the cage" at Caesars Palace. There was no subpoena of tournament records, there was no interrogation of witnesses, there was no investigation.

Before the Pro Council began the investigations into Vilas and Lendl, John McEnroe, Sr., admitted publicly that he had accepted guarantees on behalf of his son, an admission that was noted in *Tennis Magazine* very matter-of-factly. At the same time, McEnroe signed a lucrative endorsement deal with Lipton Italy and, not coincidentally, for the first time in his career he was slated to play the Italian Open. Neither matter did more than raise eyebrows.

It's easy to argue both sides of such a very complicated issue; eventually, the ATP Tour came to recognize publicly the need for a compromise.

Guarantees are a necessary evil that ultimately benefit everyone involved. Unless a tournament can draw a crowd with a big name, the tournament goes under. Tournaments go belly-up and we're *all* out of business. On the flip side, tournaments indeed went under in the double digits, but most likely because exhibitions and guarantees priced them right out of the market, making the exorbitant amounts of money involved a detriment to all but those who received them.

McEnroe opined that top players should get guarantees because they enter a tournament with the possibility of losing in the first round, walking away with virtually no prize money. This in spite of having provided the tournament with a box-office bonanza.

The argument is often made that a player guaranteed big bucks regardless of outcome might not give his best effort, might even tank. I'm not going to tell you it never happened—of course it did—however, the opposite is also true. Vilas reached the final in Rotterdam. Lendl won the title in Milan. Connors? Connors is always in a match to the death. He's incapable of less. What was it he said once? "I hate to see them win more than I hate to lose." The idea that he might not play his best is painfully ludicrous.

Like I said, it's easy to argue both sides.

I had personal experience receiving guarantees—I could name Auckland, Gstaad, Sydney, Bangkok, Vancouver, and Tokyo as places I left with bags full of U.S. cash—not to mention a few U.S. cities holding medium-sized tournaments that were willing to pay handsomely to obtain my services.

The most ludicrous turn of events in this oft-played scene went something like this: ProServ was hired by an event promoter to manage an Asian four-man special event. Naturally ProServ doesn't do this sort of thing for free, so they were paid a management fee. The promoters established a budget for ProServ to hire four players (Lendl and three others) to compete in the event. ProServ approached the players with offers for their services, noting that they were negotiating sincerely on their behalf so as to secure the best price from "the promoters" for their commitment to the event. It turns out that ProServ only used about 60 percent of the budget to pay the four players—and pocketed the rest. Of course they also collected their "commission" from each of the players. Unluckily for ProServ, some office clerk (who probably joined the ranks of the unemployed) mistakenly faxed details of the whole thing to Ivan's fax number, exposing the whole scheme.

The ensuing (no pun intended) back and forth was like something out of a *Dick and Jane* schoolbook. See ProServ. See Lendl. See ProServ exposed. See Lendl chase ProServ. See ProServ backpedal. See Lendl sue ProServ. See ProServ settle. See Lendl fire ProServ.

Circumventing the guarantee rule, "Creative Financing 101" would continue to be core curriculum among players, tournament directors, and agents throughout my era and into the next.

With the formation of the new ATP Tour in 1990, finally there was some recognition that guarantees were a necessary economic reality for mid-level tournaments. The events were consistently unable to attract the top tier of players with only the allure of the event. Logically those players could earn more money during those weeks by committing to play special events with less stress. The solution was to authorize the mid-level events to pay appearance fees as long as they were disclosed. The system finally made some sense and it continues to this day.

In the death throes of their existence, the Men's Tennis Council did manage to put an end to what was the most insidious and pervasive practice: conflict of interest. In 1985 a major antitrust lawsuit was filed by Volvo, a ProServ client. Volvo had been the major sponsor of the men's Grand Prix circuit, but Volvo sued the MIPTC after tournament title sponsorship was given to Nabisco. Both ProServ and IMG sided with Volvo.

In 1987 the United States District Court threw out Volvo's lawsuit, dismissing all the antitrust claims. In essence, the court ruling made the MIPTC the sole governing body of men's tennis. Before the ruling, IMG and ProServ had their greedy paws firmly imbedded in every aspect of the sport and the Pro Council had been virtually powerless to stop them from doing essentially anything they wanted.

One of the first rulings the MIPTC enacted after the lawsuit was dismissed was in regards to agent activity: It was determined that agents (IMG or ProServ or any similar company) could either represent players or they could own tournaments, but they could not do both. Starting with the 1989 calendar year, the new Conflict of Interest Rule went into effect.

The MIPTC was on its way out, but they had finally done something right. There was a reason why people were beginning to see things differently. His name was Hamilton Jordan.

8:

MR. JORDAN COMES
FROM WASHINGTON

IN 1976 I WAS INVITED to participate in the Robert F. Kennedy charity event at Forest Hills held prior to the U.S. Open. It was a grand event with lots of tradition (and plenty of stars from all walks of sports, entertainment, and politics) that went on for several years. Naturally the event raised millions for charity and, among other good things that came from the RFK event, it was at one of them that Arnold Schwarzenegger met Maria Shriver (of the Kennedy clan; no relation to Pam).

As a nineteen-year-old aspiring athlete with no interest in politics, I knew next to nothing about my partner for the event. I was infinitely more interested in other participants in the event, such as Farrah Fawcett and Chevy Chase. It so happened that my partner's name was Hamilton Jordan and he hailed from Georgia. He played a nice game of tennis and was very personable—and that suited me just fine. We had a successful event, enjoyed our matches, then went our separate ways.

For the next couple of years, I struggled with getting established as a tour regular, managed a few good results, won a couple of tour events in Maui, and reached the quarterfinals of Wimbledon.

Mr. Jordan served as White House Chief of Staff under President Jimmy Carter.

In 1972 the professional tennis players of the world were still basking in the newfound glory of being allowed to compete in major tournaments. But something was missing. While the professionals were technically eligible and tournaments offered prize money (amateurs declined to accept payments, the money reverting back to the tournament promoters), the old system still played favorites with entries and many was the occasion when better players were passed over in favor of the number-one-ranked representative from Uzbakistanland-ville. Other issues still bothered the players and the result was that meetings were held and voices were raised.

Locker room conversation eventually grew into formalized discussions where ideas were bandied about and eventually a plan materialized that would affect the tennis world in a way equally as significant as open tennis had done four years earlier.

The plan called for the formation of the Association of Tennis Professionals (ATP), a players' union. Conceived in the restaurant of the Los Angeles Tennis Club that spring by Donald Dell and Jack Kramer, the ATP membership would be comprised of all professional tennis players who elected to join and would set out to dictate guidelines that would govern the sport. It was, to say the least, revolutionary.

Early on, the union made it clear they meant business. In standing up for what they believed was just, the ATP often butted heads with tournament promoters and officials from the national associations. It was these individuals, collectively the ITF (International Tennis Federation), who had for years sought to promote tennis tournaments around the world without paying any prize money to the players.

Somehow I never have been able to understand how they managed to convince generation after generation of tennis players that this was a good idea. Imagine suggesting to the Rolling Stones and the Eagles that you intended to stage a series of major concerts each year. Of course you planned to sell tons of tickets and bring in lots of corporate sponsorships for the events—maybe even sell the TV rights for millions of dollars. Now, having arranged the concerts, you would be willing to let each band perform because they were among the best bands in the world. This the bands would agree to do—for free—because they were true artists and loved their craft. Seriously.

Most of the issues that came up in the early years of the ATP and its negotiations with promoters were not terribly serious. Mostly organizational and rules-oriented, but the union did show its resolve and strength when it stood toe to toe with Wimbledon in 1973. This occurred when entry was denied to Yugoslav Nicki Pilic. The issue that brought on the conflict was the Davis Cup. Pilic had elected not to play for his native Yugoslavia.

The national associations (ITF, who shared ownership of the Davis Cup competition) felt that players should be obligated to "represent their countries" by participating in the annual competition held between selected nations. The tradition dated back to when Dwight Davis donated a trophy (cup) to be awarded to each year's winners. Unlike most events, though, the Davis Cup was played in numerous venues over several weeks on the calendar, with the finals usually held in December. A commitment to play Davis Cup meant blocking out at least four weeks plus travel time. Players, of course, were not paid to play.

In the grand scheme of things, Nicki Pilic's participation was not such an important drawing card for the Davis Cup. What really mattered to the ITF was that no really big star ever got the idea that it was okay to skip the Davis Cup. Pilic made for a perfect example.

In response to Pilic's decision to skip the Davis Cup, Wimbledon supported the ITF by refusing his entry for the 1973 Championships. Battle lines were drawn: It was "us" *vs.* "them" and the players' union held to its position that no player should be forced to play in any event against his will, Davis Cup or otherwise. Wimbledon's denial of Pilic's entry was unacceptable and the ATP players threatened to strike. When Wimbledon refused to budge, the battle was on.

Tradition has always held that Wimbledon's defending champion, the "holder," opens play at 2:00 P.M. on the first Monday of the Championship.

When the 1973 Championship opened at 2:00 P.M. on the first Monday, defending champion Stan Smith wasn't there. He was joined by seventy-nine players, including four-time champion Rod Laver and three-time champion John Newcombe, who withdrew their entries, foregoing the opportunity to win tennis's most coveted prize.

However, some big names remained in the draw: Britain's Roger Taylor chose to play his national championship. Ilie Nastase crossed the picket line, *claiming* he was under orders from Romanian authorities to play. Jimmy Connors simply snubbed his nose at the ATP, which he had refused to join.

The 1973 Championship was won by Jan Kodes, who defeated Russia's Alex Metreveli in the final. All in all, though, the strike served its purpose and the players had made it clear that the ATP was a force in the game to be reckoned with. Meetings were held, compromises were made, and the players achieved their goal of independence where the Davis Cup was concerned. Ironically, the player who probably gained the most from that first ATP victory was Jimmy Connors. Even though Connors never joined the ATP and even crossed the picket line in 1973, he was able to pass up on the Davis Cup for most of his career without repercussions, thanks to the efforts of the players' union.

I should note that the Davis Cup competition has come a long way since those amateur days. Not only are the players paid for their participation in today's Davis Cup, it can often be far more lucrative than regular tournament competition. The players are also treated like royalty during the events. The U.S. Davis Cup team is sponsored by AIG, and my friend Michael Cohen, the head of all marketing for the company, works directly with Davis Cup captain Patrick McEnroe to make sure the players are given the best of everything. Credit here to the USTA where it is certainly due, because players now are eager to participate like never before.

As time passed, the ATP continued to find its place in the game. Entry systems for Grand Prix tournaments were streamlined and finally there was a central source of information for players to go to. Each week a representative from the union would remain on-site at the tournament to help players with scheduling or any other administrative concern. The ATP rep's presence at the tournaments also was a subtle reminder to the tournament promoters that fairness was expected and that tournament officials should adhere to ATP guidelines in areas like scheduling and officiating.

The maverick Connors notwithstanding, the ATP had attracted for its membership virtually every player in the game. Given the proven success of their unity (as demonstrated by the Wimbledon strike), they were in a position to dictate any terms they deemed fair and, if they chose to do so, could absolutely direct the course of professional tennis from that day forward.

It was not entirely unprecedented in the world of sports. Professional golfers had laid down the prototype with their enormously successful PGA Tour. For years the golfers had owned their own tour, granting tournament rights to promoters who followed strict guidelines, including large portions of the profits donated to charity. The golfers had even incorporated the golf teaching profession into the grand design, forming a separate entity called the PGA of America, to legitimize all levels of professional golf. It was an invitation laid before tennis players on a silver platter.

The tennis professionals passed.

Instead, they compromised—agreeing to form a new governing body for the sport called the Men's International Professional

Tennis Council (MIPTC). Nine members of the Pro Council were elected as follows: three players' representatives selected by the ATP, three representatives selected from among the national associations (ITF), and three representatives of tournament directors.

The ATP headquarters were located in Dallas, Texas, the coincidental home of Lamar Hunt's WCT, and headed by Bob Briner—yet another close ally of Donald Dell. The players' union, week in, week out, dealt primarily with issues that concerned fair play and the governance of entries, organization, and player conduct. It was the role of the ATP to structure ranking systems, entry systems, qualification systems, prize money breakdowns, point penalty systems, scoring systems, court surfaces, and tournament schedules. During the course of the year, several general ATP players' meetings were held and these topics usually dominated the meetings.

It was the responsibility of those three ATP representatives who met in separate summit meetings with the MIPTC to champion the causes of the players' union. These issues were debated in negotiations with the other six representatives. The fact that all six of the other representatives on the Pro Council were tournament directors somehow escaped major scrutiny.

At most of our general ATP player meetings, the ATP executives and leadership proudly reported to the players that a majority of the agenda items which were presented to the MIPTC as important to players were able to be passed. Thankfully, it seems, the six tournament representatives to the Pro Council consistently respected player wishes on issue after issue—rankings, qualification, player conduct, point penalties, drug testing, prize money, distribution, and so on.

There was no question but that all parties seemed unified in the belief that the game should be played at the highest level of integrity. Even proposed rule changes were agreed to without major controversy. Injury timeouts, bathroom breaks, on-court attire, and between-point time spans were among the innovative changes that came from Pro Council meetings. Other sports and industries suffered when allegations of injustice tainted the public image of their competition. Tennis had become big business with large pools of prize money available and it was very important that the world should perceive that the competition was fair. At stake was the tour's ongoing ability to attract corporate sponsorships and draw large crowds.

While all this great progress was being made, though, there was one area that saw little or no progress for years. With few exceptions, the typical level of total prize money offered at regular Grand Prix Tour events remained steady all the way into the early '80s. Corporate entertainment was emerging as a major force in the advertising world and tournaments were swimming in new sponsorships, but the payout to players saw little of the gain.

Also remaining steady was the number of events that were held in which we could play. On this subject there was considerable debate. Our leadership, sensitive to our desire to have more jobs available (by staging more events, even multiple events in the same week), pointed out to us that ticket sales and sponsorships still depended on the marquee value of the players who were scheduled for an event. Remember: Stars Sell.

Unfortunately, the tour was limited in the number of players who were considered stars by the promoters and the general public and a major disadvantage was the unwillingness of the "top players: stars" to commit themselves to more events. Bjorn Borg, Jimmy Connors, and John McEnroe were stars who consistently played in exactly twelve Grand Prix tournaments each year. Coincidentally, this was the exact number prescribed as the minimum by the ATP computer ranking system.

Players are awarded points according to tournament matches won and each player's total points are then divided by the number of tournaments played. This results in an "average" of points earned per tournament. Despite his lack of a college degree, Borg knew that a smaller denominator (tournaments played) would lend itself to a higher average—thus a higher ranking.

The result of all this is that top players limited their exposure, thus limiting the number of tournament promoters who could effectively sell tickets and sponsorships. And that meant fewer jobs for the rest of the players. The theory would eventually be put to the test by Lamar Hunt and his WCT Tour in the early '80s.

For several years, WCT had tried with declining success to act as an independent promoter of tournaments within the construct of the Grand Prix Tour. Though Hunt had been an early pioneer of professional tennis, the power structure now clearly favored Dell, ProServ, and the MIPTC, which seemed intent on increasing their influence and gradually phasing WCT out. This, of course, would ultimately result in a tournament schedule that would include more ProServ-operated events, but fewer tournaments overall.

Increasingly, the MIPTC seemed to make life more difficult for WCT. Lamar Hunt had never been a small thinker. His previous efforts in sports had resulted in the Kansas City Chiefs, the AFL, and the Super Bowl. He fashioned a response that was not subtle. He decided to raise the bar and compete head to head with the enemy. In 1982 WCT cut ties with the MIPTC and established a separate, privately operated tour that offered twenty-three events, each with a minimum purse of $300,000. New markets were opened in cities that hadn't previously seen pro tennis or that had been dropped off the Grand Prix Tour. Players enjoyed an additional $10 million of official prize money earnings that year, thanks to WCT and Lamar Hunt.

In most respects, Hunt determined to operate the new tournaments along the same guidelines set forth by the Grand Prix Tour. After all, the players had fought for years to ensure that fairness prevailed in issues such as entries, deadlines, rules, and so forth. Hunt had no desire to undermine the efforts of the ATP, only to increase the number of tournaments that were held in disparate markets around the world.

WCT's bold new venture was met head-on by the MIPTC and (strangely) the ATP. It was totally understandable that the Pro Council would oppose a collection of events that was in direct competition with its own. The reaction from the ATP staff and player representatives was totally unexpected. These "words of wisdom" were passed down from the ATP "leadership" to rank-and-file players.

1. The WCT events do not follow our entry systems to the letter and thereby threaten our integrity.
2. The WCT events do not follow our prize money breakdowns to the letter and are unjust (WCT offered a first-place prize of $100,000 and a minimum of $2,000 to first-round losers).
3. Because of these transgressions, WCT events will not be eligible for inclusion on the Grand Prix Tour and will not count for computer ranking points.

Results from WCT events were dropped from the computer! In that one stroke, the ATP had declared that it stood opposed to a promoter who was willing to offer over $10 million of income to its membership. It is hard to imagine any workers' union in the world taking such a stand. It is even harder to imagine the union membership tolerating leadership that would suggest it. The ATP was now clearly allied with the Pro Council.

With the positions clearly defined, there was no stronger trump card to be played in this battle. Touring professionals' lifeblood was the computer rankings. Nonexistent throughout history until 1973, the computer now defined the careers of most players. Eligibility for events, bonus structures in endorsement contracts, inclusion in exhibition matches or special events, and simple pride made the computer rankings the single most important force in the structure of the game.

Lawsuits were filed and WCT responded by hiring Nixdorf, a German computer concern, to offer an alternative player ranking system exactly according to ATP guidelines with one exception—results of *all* events, Grand Prix and WCT, were included for the rankings. It was Hunt's goal to convince the players (if not the ATP leadership) that WCT really did have the players' best interests at heart, and would be willing to support their overriding concerns for fair competition.

The MIPTC, always loath to share and share alike, wanted nothing less than to force Hunt and the WCT out of existence, but it stopped short of banning players who chose to play WCT events from Grand Prix or Grand Slam events.

The MIPTC had effectively done just that in 1974 when Jimmy Connors opted to play in Billie Jean King's World Team Tennis. When Nicki Pilic was banned from Wimbledon for skipping the Davis Cup, the result was an ATP boycott of Wimbledon. Connors's punishment for competing in King's rival series of events was to be banned from the French, possibly denying him the opportunity to win the Grand Slam that year, as he won Wimbledon, the U.S. Open, and the Australian Open. Connors, a non-ATP member and an outspoken opponent of Donald Dell, Jack Kramer, and the union, received no support from the ATP "leadership." The ban stood and Connors filed his own lawsuits against the French, the ATP, Dell, the MIPTC, and who knows who else.

Players who chose to play WCT events in 1982 weren't banned from Grand Prix events or Grand Slam events, but they also received no support from the ATP "leadership." In fact, Arthur Ashe spoke at several players' meetings on the subject, urging journeyman pros to support the Grand Prix Tour by boycotting WCT. He never explained how turning down enormous sums of money from Lamar Hunt would benefit any player. He also never explained how helping the Grand Prix promoters to secure their monopoly was going to enrich players.

In the end, the majority of players listened to Ashe and other "leaders" of the ATP. It cost them over $10 million in available earnings and removed any leverage the "competition" would have contributed in negotiations against the promoters of the Grand Prix Tour. By 1986 Hunt had shuttered most of his WCT Tour, maintaining selected events that included the WCT Finals in Dallas. It was not so much a financial decision as it was that he

became weary of being in constant conflict with those very players whom he intended to support.

On the subject of increased prize money (or the ongoing lack
thereof), we were told year after year that the tournament promoters were barely able to support their events. The average total
purse in the mid-'70s was $300,000 to $500,000 per week for a
top-tier Grand Prix event. Of course Grand Slams paid more. By
the mid-'80s, the average was still barely $500,000 per week.
Under the table guarantees had risen markedly, though there
were no official statistics to measure such increases. Suggestions
of mandatory increases in prize money were met with the argument that it could force some events into financial losses and
thereby threaten the overall tour. WCT's decision to cease operations only added credibility to that argument and the players
reluctantly accepted the status quo.

Another subject of much discussion during the ATP players'
meetings was the importance of ensuring that *guarantees* were out-
lawed. The leaders of the ATP, Donald Dell, Arthur Ashe, Bob
Briner, and Jack Kramer, repeatedly reminded us that tournaments should be prohibited from offering appearance fees to star
players over and above the official prize money of the event. This,
we were told, could poison the integrity of our tour and bring
into question the sacred computer ranking system. Few players
gave much thought to the fact that Donald Dell and ProServ
owned tournaments (and would be very happy to keep guarantee-
paying to a minimum).

In 1987 the ATP underwent a change in leadership and
Hamilton Jordan and I became "partners" again. I was serving as
a member of the ATP Board of Directors and Hamilton Jordan
was hired to be our executive director.

Voted by his classmates as most likely to become governor
someday, Jordan grew up in the world of politics. His grandfa-
ther, Hamilton McWhorter, had been president of the Georgia
Senate. His uncle, Clarence Jordan, a Baptist minister, founded
Koinonia (Greek for "fellowship" or "community") Farms, the

oldest continually functioning commune in the United States. It was formed near Plains, Georgia, in the '40s and promoted racial integration at a time when, to say the least, it was dangerous to do so. With an indomitable spirit, Clarence Jordan and the inhabitants of Koinonia Farms faced and survived firebombs, bullets, KKK rallies, cross-burnings, death threats, and economic boycotts. Millard Fuller got the idea for Habitat for Humanity (whose most famous volunteer is former president Jimmy Carter) from visiting Koinonia Farms.

JORDAN BEGAN LEARNING the ins and outs of the political game as a wet-behind-the-ears seventeen-year-old campaign volunteer in the state senate run of Jimmy Carter in 1962. Carter apparently had lost by a few votes, but when violations of voting rules were discovered (that age-old practice of stuffing the ballot box instigated by the local Boss Tweed), Carter challenged the results and was declared the winner.

JORDAN VOLUNTEERED AGAIN in Carter's failed gubernatorial run in 1966. In Ham Jordan, Carter recognized a natural political talent and he made Jordan his campaign manager when he ran for governor again four years later.

Carter became governor and Jordan became his executive secretary. In Georgia, when the governor is out of the state, the executive secretary becomes, in effect, the acting governor. Jordan continued to earn Carter's confidence in the way he performed this responsibility.

When Governor Carter set his sights on the White House, Hamilton Jordan orchestrated what most considered the impossible. The twenty-seven-year-old penned a politically astute seventy-two-page document which became the blueprint for one of the most brilliant and remarkable campaigns in American history. Commonplace in today's presidential campaigns, Jordan was

the first to recognize the strategic importance of the Iowa caucus
and the New Hampshire primary and made these the center point
of his architectural plan to elevate Carter to the presidency.

TO SAY THAT CARTER WAS a long shot was a gross under-
statement. Nevertheless, he stunned the political community by
taking Iowa and New Hampshire and continued the impossible
by defeating George Wallace in the South. In six months with the
Jordan strategy, Carter went from relative obscurity to his party's
nominee and from there to the highest office in the land.

In September of 1986 the ATP unceremoniously dumped
Executive Director Mike Davies. A number of issues culminated
in the sense that the union would be better served by a different
individual. As the ATP board conducted a search for the position
of executive director, some board members wanted a tennis
insider who knew every player. Others wanted a hard-nosed MBA
who knew the bottom line. An executive search firm suggested
Hamilton Jordan.

Six years after leaving the White House, a friend had submit-
ted Jordan's name to the search firm because Jordan was facing a
mountain of medical bills from his battle with cancer. At first,
Jordan was less than enthused by the prospect, but he eventually
became totally engrossed in it.

The board was less than enthused by the prospect at first as
well. The most tennis experience Jordan seemed to have was the
great "White House Tennis Controversy," where Jordan showed
up for a meeting with the President and other dignitaries wearing
tennis clothes instead of a suit. (It turns out the meeting was an
emergency, and Jordan decided it was more important to get
there fast than it was to get there properly clad.) Ray Moore, in
particular, wasn't sure Jordan was the ideal choice, but he invited
Jordan to his home in Palm Springs to get a more personal
impression.

The author of Carter's seventy-two-page campaign memo

showed up at Ray Moore's house with a leather-bound brochure he'd written called *Preliminary Thoughts: How Someone from Outside Professional Tennis Might Approach the First Year as Executive Director of the ATP.* Moore was won over and became Jordan's biggest supporter.

Jordan and four other finalists made formal presentations to the board and it wasn't even a contest. Jordan brought in charts and graphs and an easel to show his long-range plans—a mini-campaign. He was the unanimous choice to lead the ATP into the next generation.

Jordan immediately began making the rounds of the tournaments, going into locker rooms, getting to know every player personally. He became a very familiar face on the circuit. Jordan found out quickly that the players not only needed someone to know them, they needed someone to lead them.

When he was named to head the ATP at a press conference held during the Key Biscayne tournament in February 1987, it was announced that Jordan's responsibility was to develop business and marketing opportunities for professional tennis worldwide—chamber of commerce stuff. When he assumed the mantle on May 1, he found himself in the middle of a maelstrom in a political arena of a different sort.

No one could have been more ideally suited for the side he aligned himself with. Jordan was someone who could champion an underdog to victory, and finally the players' union had a leader who actually supported the players. The man who engineered the elections of a soft-spoken peanut farmer (first for governor of Georgia, then for president of the United States) took Carter populist demagoguery and rammed it right down the throat of the tennis establishment.

Just as the nation had grown tired of corrupt politicians in 1976, tennis players had grown tired of their current "leadership."

Jordan was pro-player; his interests didn't lie in contracts or endorsements or lining his own pockets. Believe it or not, most of the players' concerns weren't about money. That must have been plainly evident by their behavior toward WCT. In fact, the players' primary concerns were a general desire to command a larger voice on the Pro Council (believe me, these guys weren't thinking big; the push was to try to increase our representation on the Pro Council from three votes to four), independent representatives from the business community on the council, a playing schedule that was a little less insane, and that thing all other pro sports had—an off-season. It didn't seem to be too much to ask for, but management (the ITF and tournament promoters) held a monopoly and were quite happy to leave things as they were.

Hamilton Jordan, with the strong backing of the players, argued that the Grand Prix season—which in 1988 played over fifty weeks—was too long for the players and too confusing to attract corporate sponsorship. He also expressed growing player dissatisfaction with the increasing number of *designated* events. This related to an earlier plan by the MIPTC to increase player participation in regular tour events.

Because of the problem of top players limiting their schedules to maximize their rankings, the MIPTC had adopted a new rule/policy whereby the Pro Council held the right to assign each player to a number of "designated" events and impose a fine if the player failed to play.

Jordan put very reasonable requests before the MIPTC, and they very unreasonably turned them down time and time again. For awhile Jordan remained optimistic that reason would win the Pro Council over in time. After a couple of years of the same routine over and over again, this eventually became a source of frustration that was apparent to those of us on the board. Hamilton Jordan, former Chief of Staff of the White House, was accustomed to achieving results. Diplomacy had failed to produce the results he wanted, so Jordan did a not terribly diplomatic thing. He withdrew from the Pro Council. It was a tactic he hoped he'd never have to use, but he'd been left no alternative.

Immediate reaction was that we had given up our voice. We

had been three votes out of nine before and now we weren't even at the table. In fact, Hamilton Jordan's gambit now gave the ATP an opportunity to control its own destiny entirely by negotiating directly with the other side on an equal basis. No longer could we get outvoted at the table—because we owned the table.

It was now time for the ATP to deliver, and it was critical to the organization that we get it right. First order of business? The ATP would form its own proprietary tour, to be owned and operated by the ATP and modeled after the PGA Tour. With great expectations, we planned to announce the venture in a major press conference at the U.S. Open. Naturally the USTA refused to provide a room for a Jordan-led press conference inside the National Tennis Center, so the announcement was made in the parking lot. A major PR screwup on the part of the USTA unwittingly provided Jordan and our players with the very image that we needed: We were being left on the outside of our own sport.

Ham Jordan fired his opening volley: "The Grand Slam tournaments want to run everything and they forced us outside this great facility," This was Southern pedagoguery at its finest, a good-ol' fashioned rail stump.

Campaign buttons? Better. Our players wore and handed out sweatshirts emblazoned with ATP TOUR 1990. Political flyers? You bet. A ten-page booklet: *Tennis at the Crossroads.* The booklet listed the problems facing professional tennis and the solutions for those problems.

The majority of the top players in the world (85 of the top 100) signed contracts agreeing to play on the ATP Tour. Jimmy Connors, as expected, voiced his support for a player-run tour, but wouldn't sign a contract.

As the plan was put into action, the very first agenda item was to accept applications for tournament weeks of the new tour. Hamilton Jordan diplomatically offered that all applications would be considered, but that events with significant histories and traditions would be treated with priority. After all, it was felt that a seamless transition to the new tour would be ideal. He added one more caveat.

Jordan communicated that it was "advisable" that event promoters wishing to be included among the top tier of the new ATP Tour should commit to offer a minimum of $1 million in official prize money for the week. Tournament promoters, who had for years claimed that it was impossible to increase prize winnings, now stepped up without hesitation. Every one of them.

Players had for years been criticized for being irresponsible and having a "Take the money and run" attitude. Now it was time to pull together. We took a chance and we won the negotiation, but we still had to deliver on the tour. If we failed, we'd have no one to blame but ourselves.

When John Hancock penned his famous signature to the Declaration of Independence, he said, "We must be unanimous; there must be no pulling different ways; we must hang together." Ben Franklin responded, "Yes, we must, indeed, all hang together, or most assuredly, we shall all hang separately."

We players with unanimity had declared our independence, and while our lives didn't hang in the balance, our livelihoods certainly did. We didn't speak as eloquently, but our voices were no less fervent.

John McEnroe: "The central issue is improving the sport. Tennis is not being showcased the best it can be."

Stefan Edberg: "It's important that you have people who understand tennis running tennis. That will be the best thing for tennis."

Brad Gilbert: "The players have unity. We'll pull together. If we don't, we'll set the game back twenty years."

Andre Agassi: "Tennis needs a change. If a change isn't made, tennis just won't go anywhere. The players need to be in control because it's their lives."

Petty squabbles and career-long rivalries were set aside as we all pulled together for a common good. To a man, we all wanted not what was best for us as individuals, but what was best for the game as a whole.

Marshall Happer and the MIPTC tried one last-ditch effort to keep the players in the fold. At the beginning of December, he called his own press conference to give the players a thing or two to think about: His proposal to the players was the formation of a new MIPTC tour. There was no information offered with respect to governance—it was apparent that the new tour would still be controlled by the ITF and the event promoters—thus it really was just the same old tour with an increased offer for the players to consider.

To entice players to accept the new offer, top players would be given signing bonuses based on their rankings, payable after they fulfilled their commitment to play in twelve tournaments a year. As far as the players were concerned, the proposal was too little, too late.

Secession had been an option for some time. In our ATP board meetings, Hamilton Jordan assumed the Men's Tennis Council wouldn't even exist in the future. The Pro Council, however, wasn't quite ready to relinquish their stranglehold, and another effort was made to compromise with the players.

Still in control of the Grand Slam events, the International Tennis Federation floated this proposal to the players' union. It quietly extended invitations to players to join a new, elite ITF Tour that would begin in 1990 with its own computer ranking system. Now the catch: That ranking system would be used to determine which players would be eligible for Grand Slam events and their seedings. In effect, players would be required to compete on the new ITF Tour if they wanted to earn a ranking which would allow them to compete in the majors.

The ITF very quickly found out that behind Jordan's Southern charm and affable personality was a ruthless hell-raiser. Without qualm, he had taken on the Washington power-broker establishment, and he had absolutely no reluctance to take on the tennis establishment.

Speaker of the House Tip O'Neill referred to Hamilton Jordan as "Hannibal Jerkin" when Jordan didn't accord him extra tickets to the presidential inauguration. When Jordan recommended one of O'Neill's Massachusetts enemies for an ambassadorship, O'Neill threatened, "Do that again, son, and I'll kick your ass."

Jordan was nonplussed.

Washington muckity-mucks salivated when Jordan became the first person to face an independent counsel investigation for allegedly using cocaine at Studio 54. In the post-Watergate climate where anyone accused of anything was presumed guilty, the Grand Jury unanimously sided with Jordan in a 24–0 vote.

Did the ITF and Marshall Happer even stand a chance?

ITF attempts at intimidation were nothing for someone who had shown no fear in Washington's trial by fire. Jordan took his stand and refused to back down. The ATP Tour was a reality and it would stay that way. The players had someone who stood up for them, and they stood firmly alongside.

I wish I had been interested in politics when I first met Hamilton Jordan. I think I probably missed out on some very interesting discussions with a very intelligent man. But as player rep to the ATP Board of Directors at that most pivotal point in tennis history, I had a front row seat to watch him in action. He was a powerful advocate for the players—much more of an advocate than some former players-turned-administrators.

His effort earned him the honor of Sports Executive of the Year, along with the respect and admiration of every player. What he earned for us was immeasurable.

AUTHOR'S NOTE: Hamilton Jordan completed the term of his employment contract with the ATP, having earned for the players complete ownership of their tour and the ability to control their own destinies. When Jordan moved on to accept the CEO position at an industrial company in Georgia, the ATP found a new executive director.

By the late '90s the tournament promoters and representatives of the ITF had regained their majority control of the ATP Tour, prompting a "new" independent voice among players, led by world number-one Leyton Hewitt and Wayne Ferriera, to be formed. This new body felt it was necessary to take on issues where the players felt the ATP leadership had failed them. Seriously.

9:

PLAYING BY THE RULES

IN 1951 EARL COCHELL, a high-ranking American amateur tennis player, found out the hard way that bad behavior simply was not tolerated by the tennis establishment. The Californian was talented with a huge serve, but he had fallen behind, 1–4, after splitting the first two sets against Gardner Mulloy in the fourth round of the United States Championships at Forest Hills. In an apparent state of pique, the right-hander played the remainder of the third set left-handed and served underhanded. Among other unpleasant results, such as losing the match, this incited boos and catcalls from the crowd.

After the match, Cochell was approached by tournament referee Elsworth Davenport in the locker room. Before Davenport even had a chance to begin his reprimand, Cochell blasted him with a steamy tirade. The gist of Cochell's argument was lost in the argument, as was Davenport's attempt to deal with the situation.

Two days later, Cochell received notice from the USLTA that he was to be banned from participating in tennis for an "unspecified period" of time. It turned out to be a three-year suspension.

A generation later the first Code of Conduct was created for competitive tournament play. This was primarily because, as money had been introduced to tennis, competitive instincts ran amok, causing bad behavior to became the rule rather than the exception. The Code of Conduct was first established to govern professional tennis play in 1976. Tennis was no longer a "gentlemen's" game and two of the prime culprits were Romania's Ilie Nastase and America's Jimmy Connors.

When Nastase was eleven years old, he chased a friend through the streets of Bucharest. When he finally caught up with the boy, Nasty beat him up. Why? His victim had just taken a set from him, 6–0. Ilie never did like to lose and he especially didn't like to be shown up like that. He vowed that he'd never lose 6–0 again and that he'd do whatever was necessary to prevent it.

Once when Nastase was playing Clark Graebner, he went into his usual stalling routine when he was losing. Graebner would have none of it. In a role reversal from Nastase's childhood, Graebner simply jumped over the net and started coming after Nastase. Nastase escaped without bodily harm, but with a great deal of damage to his delicate psyche. A few games later, Ilie defaulted, saying he was too shaken up to play.

In 1975 in the Canadian Open final against Orantes after a line call that went against him, Nastase "sulked" for the rest of the match and made less than a half-assed attempt at winning. For violating the "best efforts" statue of the MIPTC Code of Conduct, he was fined $8,000, roughly his second-place winnings. Nastase had the fine reduced to $6,000 and—with semantics as skillful as the Bucharest Backfire shot he pulls when his opponent has successfully lobbed over his head—called it a donation to the Canadian junior program.

Four months later in Stockholm in the Masters against Arthur Ashe, Nastase was so obnoxious and unchecked that Ashe left the court in disgust. Because the rules simply had no provision to deal with such eventualities, the umpire was forced to disqualify Ashe. The quick-thinking tournament referee promptly stated it had "been in his mind" to default Nastase just before Ashe walked off and thus (in some version of an over-rule) made the belated call and both players were defaulted. It seems to have been a historic match in that, at least overnight, it ended with two losers. The next day Ashe was declared the winner.

However, because the Masters was played as a round-robin event, Ilie was still alive in the event, needing to lose twice in order to be eliminated from the tournament. He managed to avoid that second loss and went on to win his fourth Masters title. Ashe, influential in tennis politics and diplomatic as ever, lobbied that the sorry affair showed the need for a Code of Conduct with teeth in it, something with infractions punishable with more than just fines. He contended that, just as in other sports, our penalties should affect the score and potentially the outcome of the match. Thus was born a system of point and game penalties.

I was a spectator with IMG's Bob Kain for one of the most notoriously Nasty matches in U.S. Open history—the second-round night match between Ilie Nastase and John McEnroe. Kain and I saw the same match, but we walked away with two totally disparate views. Kain, the great image maker, saw a ratings bonanza. I saw the final nail in the coffin of the gentlemen's game.

The year 1979 marked Nastase's first appearance at Flushing Meadows, missing out on the inaugural year in one of his many suspensions. For Ilie's opening act (first round), he performed a striptease. Nastase was leading Leo Palin in the first round, 7–5, 6–5, but the humidity was overbearing, and Ilie found himself dripping with perspiration in the clammy heat. On the change-over, Nastase very loudly said, "Excuse me, everybody," then proceeded to drop his sweat-soaked shorts. He kicked them away with a laugh, then donned a fresh pair. He went on to win the match, once more demonstrating his knack for combining exquisite tennis with burlesque. At the press conference afterward Ilie quipped, "A lot of ladies here, so I leave my pants on." Then he looked very pointedly at one woman reporter and queried her: "You want my pants on or off?"

Nastase had a cartoon taped on his locker. On one panel of the cartoon, a ticket booth featured a sign that said NOW SHOWING NASTASE VS. MCENROE. The next panel said THIS MATCH IS RATED R. NO ONE UNDER 17 ADMITTED WITHOUT A PARENT OR GUARDIAN. Nastase loved that cartoon and with his victory over Palin and McEnroe's pummeling of Pavel Slozil, the show was on.

Newspapers had trumpeted the occasion; tournament officials had scheduled it for the second match Thursday evening, August 30, a 9:00 P.M. start.

It was staged almost as if it were a huge publicity stunt; an exhibition by the game's best exhibitionists. Imagine the worst and it was worse than that. Nasty was nasty, Mac was nasty, the crowd was nasty, and the aftertaste was—well, nasty.

Tournament officials anticipated "trouble," and they gave the next-to-impossible task of maintaining law and order on the court to the extremely competent and more importantly extremely patient Frank Hammond, a highly qualified chair umpire with a knack for handling testy tennis players. There was more "trouble" than anyone knew what to do with.

Nastase, whose career was in decline, used every trick in his repertoire to psych the rising young tennis star. At one point, Nastase insisted on stopping the match and telephoned air-traffic control at La Guardia and asked if the planes could be diverted because they were making too much noise. He clowned around in typical Ilie fashion, mocking McEnroe's stalling and incessant questioning of line calls. In every language he was fluent in, he cursed, disputed line calls, and hurled insults across the net at his opponent. McEnroe, no slouch when it comes to invective, replied in kind.

While the match degenerated with Mac and Nasty increasing each other's ante in the gamesmanship stakes, an unruly and decidedly pro-Nastase New York crowd of ten thousand got involved and the booing began. The booing was the least of it. They began throwing paper cups, soda cans, beer cans, and a few invectives of their own. Egged on by the crowd, who were throwing eggs and tomatoes as well as insults, Nastase became impossible to control.

With McEnroe leading, 6–4, 6–4, 2–1, Hammond ordered Mac to serve in an attempt to rein in Nastase and the crowd. Mac served before Nastase was ready and Hammond called it 15–0. Let the games begin.

Nastase protested the "quick serve." Before he was done "protesting," Hammond had slapped him with a game penalty.

Nastase was ordered to serve 1–3, and he refused, instead pacing the baseline as Hammond literally pleaded with him to play on. The crowd was shouting their version of the score boisterously, *"Two-one! Two-one!"*

After several minutes delay, referee Mike Blanchard signaled for Hammond to put Nastase on the clock, giving him thirty seconds to serve or be defaulted. A minute elapsed and nothing happened, so Hammond announced, "Game, set, and match to McEnroe!"

The crowd erupted and for eighteen minutes there was mob rule. Fights broke out in the crowd and an invasion of the court seemed imminent. Police and security guards were summoned. With the crowd in a frenzy and reporters scurrying around to describe the unfolding scene, one sports writer quipped sardonically that air-traffic control had called the tennis center and asked if Mr. Nastase could get the crowd to keep the noise down because they couldn't hear the planes.

At this point the match had gotten so out of control that the tournament director, Bill Talbert, was summoned. After some discussion, Talbert offered his ruling that Nastase should be reinstated (as he feared a riot might occur) and instead it was Frank Hammond who should be removed. Mike Blanchard himself replaced Hammond in the chair and the match resumed.

Well after midnight, McEnroe finally managed to win the

match in four sets and possibly became the first player ever to win the same match twice. He went on to win his first U.S. Open with a victory over Vitas Gerulaitis in the final.

At one point in the match, Nastase made a vain plea with the chair to have some penalty imposed on his opponent. He pleaded, "McEnroe keeps calling me son of a bitch. Make him call me 'Mr. Son of a Bitch.'"

During the two weeks of the 1979 U.S. Open, only one person connected with the game had their picture on the front page of the *New York Post* three different days. That person was the second-round loser in men's singles: Ilie Nastase.

The tournament in general that year was a lesson to all the players in how star power and showbiz had infiltrated the game. The trailer that served as the tournament office practically reeked with the stench of favoritism.

Certainly many decisions have been made over the years in conducting major sporting events that were not entirely fair to all the competitors. It sometimes is simply impossible to accommodate everyone equally, especially with factors such as weather and the fact that players compete in several divisions (singles, doubles, mixed) and all must be prioritized. However, some actions are simply unjustified.

It defied all reason that the quarterfinal match between Jimmy Connors and Patrick DuPre should be scheduled on Stadium Court less than twenty-four hours after DuPre finished a five-set marathon against Harold Solomon. That match ended with DuPre cramping on match point and vomiting in the locker room afterward.

Certainly there was no need to rush the quarterfinals. Traditionally, the semifinals of the U.S. Open are held on Saturday (to accommodate CBS and forcing back-to-back semis and finals). This means that the tournament has twelve days from the first Monday to complete the five rounds leading up to the semis. Even if matches are held every other day, it still leaves two extra days off and, even with rain, there is little reason for any matches to be played back to back.

Unless.

It eventually came to light that Connors had paid the tournament committee a visit. When Connors came to the tournament office to find out when he would play DuPre, he was offered his choice: the next afternoon or the following night. Connors, never one to look a gift horse in the mouth, opted for the afternoon match, which would give him an extra day's rest if he made it to the semifinals—as if there were any doubt.

DuPre not only didn't expect the scheduling, he wasn't even informed of it. On the morning of the match, Pat's wife, Darcy, was thumbing through a local newspaper while Pat slept off his marathon match with Solomon, and she just happened to spot Pat's name scheduled to face Connors in a few hours. Darcy woke Pat from a deep slumber and they raced from the hotel to Flushing Meadows in time for the match, but naturally Connors coasted by a very bitter, very weary opponent.

Connors owned the U.S. Open. If you don't believe it, just ask him.

The scheduling roulette afflicted not just men's singles, but also women's singles, doubles play for both, and mixed doubles as well. I fell in the first round to Tomas Smid in five sets in the men's singles, but I paired quite successfully in mixed doubles with my friend Martina Navratilova. We reached the semifinals, but when we showed to play Frew McMillan and Betty Stove, we found we had been defaulted for not showing in time. In this case, the scheduled start of the match had been changed without anyone bothering to inform us. On discovering our fate, I accompanied Martina, who was in tears, distraught, to the tournament trailers and met for at least an hour with the officials to appeal the default. They eventually reconsidered, and the match was allowed to be played. Though Martina and I won the case in getting ourselves reinstated, we unfortunately lost the match.

Even in the U.S. Open, an event that should be able to get by on its own strength without sucking up to the stars, favoritism is the rule rather than the exception. I suppose it's a fact of life that we all get used to, but the truth is that even the USTA answers to higher powers. Television ratings are king and the actions of the tournament officials are understandable if they are seen in the light of hoping for a bonanza final between Connors and McEnroe. It is a fact that ratings depend on star power. Yearly statistics on the Open, Wimbledon, the World Series, and even the Super Bowl demonstrate that people decide to watch based on who's playing.

That said, the realities don't necessarily lend themselves to greater fairness in implementing the rules.

Case in point is that neither McEnroe nor Nastase, whose actions that infamous night were way beyond anything antici- pated by the Code of Conduct, got the hook. The tournament couldn't afford to yank either of them. Frankly, had either Nastase or McEnroe been some no-name journeyman exhibiting his boor- ish behavior before a handful of spectators on some far-flung out- lying court, he would have found himself banished to the showers early in the match with a notice posted for all to see of just how infractions would not be tolerated.

But when you're a star with huge drawing power playing before a sizable crowd in a televised event, codes of conduct are subject to a more lenient interpretation. After all, tennis is show- biz and of course "The show must go on." The star's not going to get jerked off the stage just for improvising his script.

Mac flaunted impropriety in the face of every opponent he ever faced throughout his career. He'll tell you that fans like to see a player argue with the umpire or a linesman or the other player or a spectator; that it's exciting, like a batter storming the mound and the ensuing bench-clearing brawl. He claims he was just giving everyone what they want to see. But unlike baseball players, his actions not only weren't spontaneous but they were flagrantly staged and so very opportune and most assuredly he wasn't tossed from the game or subject to an auto- matic suspension.

Through years and years of flaunting every rule he could think of, it was not until 1990 that McEnroe was ever defaulted from a match. Conventional wisdom was that by then the game had moved beyond John and, basically, the Grand Slams finally found that he was not indispensable. The moment of truth came at the Australian Open and Mac, as usual, was in grand style. Also as usual, he was in complete control. He knew exactly how far he could go with each strike and just what it would take to draw the fourth and decisive one. He only made one tiny miscalculation. The new ATP Tour had enacted a three-strikes rule effective January 1. Any player cited for unsportsmanlike conduct three times in a match must be disqualified.

Mac thought the Australian Open was being played under the previous year's rule, which allowed him that pivotal fourth strike. Oops, dead wrong.

Playing against Sweden's Mikael Pernfors, the 1984 and 1985 NCAA champ for the University of Georgia, McEnroe had split the first two sets in the fourth-round match. He had a commanding lead in the third set, but after a lineswoman made a close call in Pernfors's favor, Mac walked up to her and glared for several seconds. Chair umpire Gerry Armstrong slapped him with a warning for unsportsmanlike conduct.

Strike One.

In the fourth set, Pernfors was coming on strong, so of course Mac began to pour it on. When he heard a baby crying in the stands, Mac snapped, "Get it a drink, for Christ's sake!"

It didn't win Mac any brownie points. Armstrong asked the mother to leave, which she did. Moments later, with Mac serving 2–3, 30–30, he hit a shot wide. He threw down his racket, which cracked audibly when it bounced on the synthetic surface. Armstrong cited Mac for "racket abuse" and docked him a penalty point.

Srike Two.

McEnroe stared long and hard at Armstrong and slowly walked to the chair. He knew his racket was cracked, but he intended to continue play with it so that the point penalty would be unjustified. Armstrong was unswayed by John's argument, so Mac called the chief of supervisors, Ken Farrar, out to the court. Farrar, Armstrong, and tournament referee Peter Bellenger listened patiently as Mac argued his case. Farrar then ruled that the point penalty would stand and the group dispersed. Armstrong announced, "Let's play," and Mac, always eager to get the last word in, fired an obscene parting shot at Farrar.

Strike Three. You're Out. You're Gone.

The crowd was incensed over the default, just as they had been when Nastase was defaulted at the '79 Open, but this time the decision stood, despite fan calls for Mac's return. Tournament officials were totally in agreement.

For thirteen years, Mac had gotten away with murder on the circuit. So convinced of his own righteousness, so ensconced in his own megalomania, he wanted to impose his will on everyone. Not content to play his opponent, he insisted on calling the lines, lecturing umpires, chastising spectators, vilifying journalists, and defying the rules.

Linesmen are asked every week to perform the thankless and near-impossible task of judging whether tennis balls traveling at speeds faster than 100 miles an hour landed just in front of, on, or just beyond lines two inches wide. It's nearly impossible for any human being to call a fast shot that lands close to the line. There's no avoiding the fact that there are going to be some bad calls.

Not only can players argue line calls, they also can have linespersons removed. Can you imagine a baseball player asking for and receiving a new umpire after he'd been called out on strikes? Not likely. If a baseball player even enters into a "serious disagreement" with the ump over a ball or strike call, he gets tossed—star or not—and most assuredly the umpire will still be in the game.

Bjorn Borg had a linesman removed in Memphis when twice called for a footfault. Ivan Lendl had a linesman removed at the

Spectrum at Philadelphia's United States Pro Indoor after a call he didn't like in a match against Wojtek Fibak.

Many umpires, including Frank Hammond, claimed that certain players (he cited John McEnroe as an example) could even name their own linesmen or umpires as a condition of playing the tournament and that tournament directors tried to pressure officials into relaxing the rules for stars.

In an attempt to curb the resulting bad dialogue that ensued between players and linesmen, the Overrule Rule was enacted in 1978. It quickly became one of the most controversial issues in the game.

The Overrule Rule reads as follows in the MIPTC rules supplement:

> The chair umpire may overrule a linesman only in the case of a *clear* mistake by the linesman and only if the overrule is made *promptly* after the mistake is made, or if the chair determines that the clear mistake made by a linesman hindered an opponent.

The rule mandating a fine for skipping press conferences could be named the Gerulaitis clause, so often did he manage to avoid their calling. And somewhere a bronze sculpture must immortalize Nastase as prompting the Visible Obscenity Rule (the sculpture obviously would display Ilie's talented middle finger). Most assuredly, the Overrule Rule was engraved with John McEnroe's name on it. It was a gilded invitation to Mac that allowed every call to be reviewed, questioned, and perhaps reversed. The Overrule Rule simply legalized John's many conversations between himself and the chair.

Bud Collins tried to perform what could have been one of the greatest services in all of mankind when McEnroe was still an amateur. Mac nearly beat Connors in a match at the U.S. Pro tournament in Boston in August 1977, along the way demonstrating that he was also as adept as Connors in the "behaving badly" category. Collins, a respected sports columnist for the *Boston Globe* and prominent TV tennis commentator, was moved to lecture the talented youngster on the subject of sportsmanship.

Collins was a traditionalist and had great respect for the previous generation's top players. A great deal of that respect was based on the values demonstrated by Laver, Rosewall, Smith, Ashe, Newcombe, Roche, and on and on. The respect was mutual, as Collins treated players professionally in his reporting and commentary. Collins was also a collaborater on one of the best books to be published on the sport: *The Education of a Tennis Professional* by Rod Laver and Collins.

On that summer day in Boston, Collins reminded McEnroe of the great players like Laver and Rosewall and stressed that they would never have resorted to such behavior. Expectedly, Mac's response was contrite, claiming that Laver was his role model and promising that it would never happen again.

By 1981 McEnroe had easily supplanted Nastase as the court's reigning bad boy, but there really is no comparing their actions. Ilie could drag out his whole repertoire and be indisputably outlandish, but it was always usually spontaneous. His intent was less likely a direct attempt to throw off his opponent's concentration. If anything, the person bothered the most was probably Ilie himself. Evidence shows that in most cases where Nastase truly got out of control, his tennis suffered and he wound up playing worse afterward, usually losing the match.

Mac's behavior, on the other hand, was a weapon he wielded against his opponent. He simply chose opportune moments to use it. In London in 1981, it became part of our national consciousness.

The Stella Artois Championship at Queen's Club, Baron's Court, London, was a major part of most players' preparation for Wimbledon. In that precious two weeks between the French Open on red clay and Wimbledon on slick grass, Queen's was the best opportunity to get match-tough and get used to the grass at the same time. The event was efficiently run for years by Clive

Bernstein (now deceased) and scheduled by Cheslav Spychala (or "Spike," as he was known to every player in the field).

One of the best things about playing the event at Queen's was that those players who did compete were then afforded unlimited grass court practice throughout the rest of Wimbledon. This technically should count as an illegal *guarantee* offered by the event as incentive to play but . . . just kidding. Actually the arrangement also proved invaluable every year because Queen's also maintains several indoor courts and, surprisingly for a place that is famous for its rain, the city has very few indoor courts.

Well, in this particular year Queen's offered a generous preview of what we could expect from Mac at Wimbledon. In the quarterfinals, he had a bad-tempered confrontation with Hank Pfister (who was only a shade friendlier with Mac than I was) and a bad-tempered confrontation with umpire Ian Stirk when he was cited for "audible obscenity." During his defeat of Brian Gottfried in the final, he cursed a lineswoman, hit a ball at her, and mercilessly baited chair umpire Georgina Clark.

Come Wimbledon, the inevitable happened almost immediately. It was on Court One in the first round against the left-handed twin Tom Gullikson. Gullikson went ahead, 4–3, in the first set, and when you get ahead of Mac, the very predictable happens.

After Mac's serve was called long, the most memorable tirade in the history of tennis began with: "Chalk flew!"

When John drew a warning from chair umpire Edward James, a new catchphrase was born: "You cannot be serious!" Umpire James was in fact serious and penalized Mac a point to demonstrate just how serious he was.

Mac then *demanded* to see tournament referee Fred Hoyles. He four-lettered Hoyles up and down the baseline and when Hoyles upheld the umpire's penalty, Mac uttered his second most famous line: "You are the absolute pits of the world!"

For all the fireworks, you might have expected a hard-fought match. Maybe even one where John was in danger of losing. Not this time. Mac ended his first round against Gullikson, winning in straight sets. He ended his first round against the Wimbledon officials with a $1,500 fine, the first fine assessed a player for bad behavior in the tournament's 104-year history.

The $1,500 was pocket change to Mac, and besides, it was early in the tournament. He had plenty more opportunity in later rounds with other players and other officials. In a doubles match with Peter Fleming against Vijay and Anand Amritraj, Mac accused a dark-skinned linesman who happened to be wearing a turban of being "biased." Vijay, one of our sport's best ambassadors, said that if he had to act like McEnroe to win the championship, he wouldn't want it.

For "aggravated behavior" (maybe they were aggravated that Mac hadn't learned his lesson the first time), the All England Club recommended an additional fine of $2,500.

John McEnroe's semifinal match against Australian Rod Frawley held more infamy than the opening round against Tom Gullikson and the already famous "You cannot be serious!" line. Frawley, ranked about 110 at the time, figured since he had reached the semifinals, that more than entitled him to break Mac's serve in the first game.

The first game of the match! How anybody gets out of hand in the first game of a match I don't know, but well, this was McEnroe, and . . . When the Centre Court crowd showed their appreciation of Frawley's play, Mac called them "vultures." When that prompted a conduct warning from the chair umpire, Mac called umpire George Grimes "a disgrace to mankind." When that drew a point penalty from Grimes, Mac called Fred Hoyles out for another meeting.

After the match, Frawley called Mac out for another meeting. The semifinal round had been strife-ridden and foul-humored. Mac questioned a record seventeen calls, and he did so with language so obscene that Lady Di actually left the Royal Box. This caused one reporter to quip, "The wedding's off; her ears are no longer virgin."

Frawley wanted to go another round—in the locker room. It didn't matter to him that with Wimbledon's class stratification system of assignments he had been relegated to the inferior B Locker Room at the back of the grounds. The Prince of Wails (aka Johnny Mac) would be found at the elite A Locker Room in the clubhouse, so that was where Frawley headed. His fist was on a collision course with Mac's face.

Somebody stopped Frawley's fist in midair. It wasn't so much that Mac was surrounded by friends as it was that Frawley was one of the good guys. His Aussie buddies stepped in to protect him, not Mac. If that fist had connected, Frawley would have been the one in trouble—one of the unfortunate injustices of life.

The All England Lawn Tennis & Croquet Club felt much the same. For over a century, one of the great traditions of Wimbledon is that each year's champion is offered an honorary membership to the club. At tournament's end, Mac became the only champion in that long list of winners not to be offered the honorary membership. The Wimbledon tournament committee instead fired off a letter to the Pro Council recommending a $10,000 fine, the maximum allowable under the Code of Conduct and an amount that carried with it a suspension.

When Marshall Happer announced that McEnroe would be fined $5,000, the All England Club was incensed. McEnroe was incensed as well and demanded, as prescribed by the rules, a three-man board of arbitration to review the case. By some other strange course of events, the rules also held that the "accused" was also entitled to appoint, as one of the three, any person of his choosing. With John's right to appoint one member, he chose the longtime head of the Port Washington Tennis Academy, Harry Hopman.

The vote was 2–1, Hopman siding with McEnroe. After a long

and respected career, it was sad to see Hopman's integrity appear to be compromised.

In order for the verdict to be upheld, the vote had to be unanimous. McEnroe paid no fine. He served no suspension. The game went on.

10:

GIVING SOMETHING BACK TO THE GAME

IN WRITING THIS, I realize that I am very obviously riding the fence when it comes to on-court behavior. First, I am in no position to claim that I always behaved like Borg or Laver when things went against me during a match. To be sure, I wish I had been able to do just that because, unlike McEnroe, my own outbursts usually left me drained and frustrated, unable to regain my form.

I also know that I am mostly critical (for their outbursts) of the very same players who defined our era in terms of magnetic personalities and the ability to draw crowds. Thus the title of this chapter is as ironic as it is sarcastic. For their tantrums, these larger-than-life superstars paid monetary fines that totaled more than some other players' total earnings. These same players were also responsible for dramatic increases in tickets sold and TV viewership, resulting in more prize money and larger sponsorships.

As I reviewed this chapter, my overriding sense was that, while the players are clearly the perpetrators of each incident, one can hardly blame them for acting as they did. After all, there was no particular reason offered to dissuade them from it, and each case only served to make them more and more notable.

If it was to be that such behavior should be stifled, responsibility fell not on the players to govern themselves, but on the leadership of the sport to enforce rules that were already on the books.

The Men's International Professional Tennis Council in their infinite wisdom were moved to rewrite the Code of Conduct for 1982 to make the penalties for misbehavior stiffer. Players were skeptical that the new code would be any more a deterrent to Mac's repeat offenses than the old code. As long as McEnroe was a tournament drawing card, he was above the rules—any rules. Unfortunately, that was an economic law that we all recognized and could do nothing about. Any attempts to subject Mac to law and order generally created lawlessness and disorder.

Mac had ended 1981 much as you'd expect, within a few hundred dollars of the twenty-one-day suspension limit. His appearance in London at Benson and Hedges Wembley in November rubbed salt into the wound he had inflicted upon England at Wimbledon. In the final, he and his opponent, none other than Jimmy Connors, were at their devastating worst. Connors was fined $400 for shouting an obscenity on court. Mac had a running battle with umpire John Parry and tournament referee Colin Hess. He was fined $350 for "racket abuse" and "abuse of the umpire's chair" (put the two together) and another $350 for "ball abuse" when he hit one onto the roof. Those fines were enough to put Mac over the limit, facing suspension yet again.

At Wimbledon 1982, Rod Frawley was still frothing at the bit. Several times he had watched the videotape of his match with McEnroe. Of the seventeen times Mac had questioned calls, two of them had been close enough to garner a closer look—two. It was the prime example of what all Mac's opponents had come to realize; he didn't argue calls because he was in some complex "rage for perfection," but for gamesmanship pure and simple.

Mac was still frothing at the bit because after twelve months he still hadn't gotten the trophies he felt he was entitled to. He was also frothing because he had lost to Connors in the final at

Queen's Club. Connors was frothing at the bit to win Wimbledon, something he hadn't done since 1974.

After Mac had gotten away with all the disgraceful behavior he exhibited at Wimbledon in 1981, the All England Club seemed to realize that when it came to McEnroe no bad deed goes punished. Throughout his matches in '82, John launched verbal assaults with impunity, so eventually some of the players, realizing they would get no help from the officials, decided to handle Mac themselves.

Hank Pfister hadn't forgotten his match with McEnroe at Queen's in '81. (Players tended to have long memories when it came to Mac.) I'm sure a doubles match Pfister had with Mac in Maui in 1980 was still fresh in his memory banks as well. Mac flat out taunted Pfister, opining that he was getting "worked up" in the doubles match because he couldn't win in singles anymore. I'm sure Pfister remembered that, and I'm also sure he remembered the real reason he was "worked up"—because Mac was pulling his usual stunts. When they met again in the fourth round at Wimbledon, Pfister had just a tiny bit of retribution playing the game in a way Mac was sure to understand.

Mac argued vociferously with the chair when a let wasn't called, but nothing he said or did swayed the umpire or the netcord judge. Hank wasn't the least bit disconcerted by Mac's well-worn ploy. From the far end of the court, Pfister ever-so-sweetly said, "I heard it, John." When John beseechingly turned to Hank and asked, "Wanna play two?" Hank got this huge grin on his face and said, "Well, since you asked so nicely. . . . No!" Mac went on to win the match, but that wouldn't be the last time in the tournament a player decided to give Mac what he had coming to him.

In a semifinal doubles match that pitted McEnroe and Fleming against Steve Denton and Kevin Curren, McEnroe questioned so many calls it was patently clear to Denton and Curren that it was a deliberate attempt to upset them and throw off their play.

Despite their complaints, Mac didn't draw any warnings or penalties. Off court, he did.

Denton literally chased Mac into the locker room, slammed the door behind him, and lunged. They were quickly separated, but unlike the case with Frawley, Denton got a few blows in first. Denton was burly and, as you may recall, a Texan. Enough said.

What happens when an irresistible force meets an immovable object? It's either an off-court confrontation between Denton and McEnroe or an on-court confrontation between McEnroe and Connors.

In that year's final of the "gentlemen's" singles, Mac played his heart out, flew into rages, demeaned linesmen, umpires, and ball boys, screamed obscenities, and lost anyway. Connors dethroned McEnroe, 6–3, 6–3, 7–6, 7–6, 6–4.

McEnroe came off court after losing his singles title and threatened to default in doubles unless it was reduced to two out of three sets. Of course, it was reduced to two out of three sets. Do you see a pattern here? As bad as John's conduct was, I have to point out that the real culprits through all the years were the authorities. It's not as though there weren't rules in place to deal with his shtick. It's not as though there was some question as to how to deal with it. Like always, the right course of action was all too clear and . . . ? They passed.

On this day Mac asked for preferential treatment and he got it. But this time it came back to bite him in the ass. Peter McNamara and Paul McNamee dispatched McEnroe and Fleming in forty-nine minutes, 6–3, 6–2.

At this point it should be mentioned that bad behavior was not the exclusive domain of McEnroe, Connors, and Nastase. Quite a few other players managed to get in a few good licks as well. Many of these, I'm sure, were genuine tantrums arising out of real frustration. After all, these players, though talented, were also human with great desires and strong emotions.

On the other hand, I witnessed quite a number that just didn't seem to be consistent with the players' decorum. Is it possible that these players were hoping that if they behaved like McEnroe, maybe they'd win like him, too?

In the qualifying rounds of the Italian Open in 1982, Marzio Miloro was fined $200 because, as his citation read, he ". . . got into a shouting match with a spectator, jumped over the fence into the stands and chased spectator up nine rows, shouting at him; they got into 'face to face' argument. Player returned to court, continued shouting at spectator." The spectator turned out to be his father.

In early 1983, Buster Mottram and Van Winitsky played in an exhibition match at a resort hotel on the Caribbean island of Antigua. When a spectator started heckling Winitsky, he charged into the crowd and struck the spectator. Marshall Happer launched an investigation of the incident. Even though this had occurred at a non-Grand Prix event, Happer ruled that Winitsky had violated the Grand Prix rule against conduct severely detrimental to tennis. Winitsky was suspended for thirty-five days.

If you wonder what, if anything, would have happened to Miloro or Winitsky had they been a star, look no further than the U.S. Open that same year. In the first round at Flushing Meadows, McEnroe was scheduled to play Trey Waltke, my friend and neighbor. Trey was a successful junior player and had managed quite a number of strong performances on the tour.

More importantly, though, Trey had upset Mac both times they had played as professionals. From the start, it was destined to be a dogfight. For five sets, Waltke played coolly and very effectively, letting nothing upset him. Mac let everything upset him. John prevailed in the end, but he didn't come out unscarred.

During that single match, he amassed fines of $1,850: $350 for "ball abuse" when he slammed one at the north end boxes, nearly decapitating front row regular Alan King; $500 for "umpire abuse," telling chair umpire Stu Saphire, "You stink!"; and $1,000 for "spectator abuse."

Apparently two courtside spectators were clapping a little too enthusiastically for Waltke. McEnroe cursed them, threw a handful of sawdust that ended up in their faces, and allegedly challenged one to a fistfight. The fines put Mac within $200 of the $7,500 per year limit where a mandatory suspension of twenty-one days would kick in.

Now for a little perspective: For a year's cumulative crimes, Mac would face a suspension that was fourteen days less than the punishment doled out to Van Winitsky for a single incident. As for the same "conduct," attacking a spectator, not just in a Grand Prix event but in a Grand Slam event, Marshall Happer determined that in Mac's case it apparently didn't constitute "conduct severely detrimental to tennis."

During the fortnight at Wimbledon, Jimmy Connors was fined $500 for "visible obscenity." Mark Edmondson was debited $750 for "abuse of a linesman."

John McEnroe kindly neglected to wrap his racket around an umpire's neck or suggest an anatomical impossibility to a linesperson. His behavior at Queen's Club had him on notice. In the finals there, he called the chair umpire an "idiot" and a "moron." Amazingly, John took offense when his opponent and friend, Leif Shiras, looked amused at his outburst. On the next changeover, Mac pointed a finger at him and warned, "I'm not going to take that crap from you."

England got off lucky. It was the French Open in 1984 where Mac was at his historic and hysteric worst. In the third round, Mac's friend Mel Purcell broke out to an early lead, at which point Mac broke into complaints about the condition of the court. Mac refused to continue the match unless the maintenance people came out to tend to the clay. They did. Any chance they would have extended the same courtesy if Mel Purcell had issued the request?

For the entire half hour that he waited in the locker room for his dictum to be carried out, Mac ranted about how stupid the French were. When he and Purcell took the court again, Purcell had totally lost his momentum and Mac beat him easily.

While beating Jimmy Connors in the semifinals, Mac was so rude and obnoxious that Connors, the progenitor of rude and obnoxious, yelled at him, "Shut up! Grow up! I've got a son your age!"

In the final, it was put up or shut up. Ivan Lendl shut him up. He broke McEnroe's match win streak at forty-five. After losing to Lendl in five sets despite taking the first two sets, McEnroe swiped his racket in the vicinity of a French cameraman and cracked his lens, which led to the cameraman apparently cutting one of his fingers in the process. McEnroe wasn't a gracious loser.

In September McEnroe pulled a $2,000 fine for uttering an obscenity at Nora McCabe, a reporter for the *Toronto Globe and Mail*, during the Players' Invitational in Toronto the month before. The fine for abusing a reporter was unprecedented and came about after she filed an official complaint with the Pro Council.

In October McEnroe crossed the $7,500 line and pulled a three-week sit-down. He blew it off, saying he "needed a rest anyway."

For all of his antics, fines, and suspensions, one might think that McEnroe was having a difficult year. Far from it. In fact, he was having the best year of his career.

John McEnroe ended 1984 having won nine of eleven Grand Prix events and seventy-eight of eighty Grand Prix matches, losing only to Ivan Lendl in the final of the French Open and Vijay Amritraj in the first round of the ATP Championship in Cincinnati. He received the $600,000 bonus for finishing first in the Grand Prix standings, pushing his "official" 1984 tournament earnings to $1.289 million and naturally ended the year with the world number one.

He also ended 1984 facing a forty-two-day suspension, which was predictably reduced to twenty-one days. His $2,100 in assessed fines ($350 for "ball abuse"; $750 for "abuse of official"; and $1,000 for "unsportsmanlike conduct") for three counts of misbehavior in the semifinal match against Anders Jarryd in the Stockholm Open pushed his fines over the $7,500 in a twelve-month period limit. Clearly suffering his own version of the Stockholm Syndrome, Mac smashed a courtside tray of drinks after not getting a response from the umpire when he screamed out yet another Mac immortal line: "Answer the question, jerk! Answer the question!"

In the November 1984 issue of *Tennis Magazine*, an article entitled "Mac the Mouth" called for "the sports authorities simply to do what pro tennis' rules say they can. Suspend a player for a year when his pattern of misconduct violates established guidelines." A week after the issue hit the newsstands, Mac unleashed that memorable tennis tantrum at the Stockholm Open. The Pro Council had their chance to impose that one-year suspension, or even the forty-two-day suspension. Instead McEnroe pulled yet another three-week stint. Did anybody ever really think that the tennis authorities might actually suspend the biggest drawing card in the game for a whole year? Seriously?

Soon after his suspension ran out, Mac returned to Sweden with Jimmy Connors for the Davis Cup finals. At the beginning of 1984, I was the third-highest-ranked American behind McEnroe and Connors. I thought for sure a Davis Cup slot was mine. I was wrong.

To his credit McEnroe always played; but Connors, pledging allegiance only to Connors, snubbed his nose at representing country over self. That was the self-evident picture. The story behind the scenes was entirely different. Arthur Ashe had decided he was going to push and push hard to get Connors to play. He had just the right ally: Jimmy's newly hired manager and Ashe's agent, Donald Dell.

Dell convinced "What's in it for me?" Connors that the Davis Cup would be another notch in his holster. Forget patriotism; forget prestige. Play to complete your résumé. Connors and McEnroe became a team, and it was nothing short of disastrous. Ashe had imagined a "Dream Team," but what he got was a nightmare. As difficult as it is to picture Scanlon and McEnroe as a team, even we would have gotten along better than McEnroe and Connors.

In Sweden Mac was just his churlish disagreeable self. Connors made him look like an altar boy by comparison. Every bit of vitriol and vileness he could muster spewed forth against umpire George Grimes in a match against Mats Wilander. Connors called him a few choice unprintable names, resulting in a point penalty, a game penalty, and a $2,000 fine. Because it was a Davis Cup final, he didn't pull a default.

Sponsors, however, threatened to pull the plug on the Davis Cup unless something was done to curb the behavior of the "ugly Americans." So the United States Tennis Association (USTA) decided to require future Davis Cup players to sign an agreement promising not to misbehave. They must "act with courtesy and civility towards competitors, officials, and spectators." McEnroe claimed to have been insulted by the request after so many years of loyalty. He refused to sign the agreement and was invited to play anyway.

In 1985 McEnroe was asked to resign from Queen's Club after a complaint about his behavior. The complaint? John was practicing on one of the indoor courts during the winter—during an off-week away from his tournament schedule. When his allotted time expired, the foursome who had reserved the court for the next hour politely entered the court and watched the world number one play a few more points. Soon, however, it became clear that Mac had no intention of stopping and when they gently suggested (as elderly British ladies do) that they'd like to play, they instead got one of Mac's famous tantrums.

On notification by the club's directors, he refused to relinquish his membership, calling the request "unwarranted." Queen's Club expelled him.

In 1985 Mac took an extended break from the game. It was left to Connors to carry the banner of exemplary sportsmanship. In the semifinals of the Lipton Players' International in Boca

Raton on February 21, 1986, Connors, still irate over a line call in the second set that he had vehemently protested to no avail, protested what he thought was a bad line call in the sixth game of the fifth set. That call gave Ivan Lendl a 3–2, 40–0 lead. Umpire Jeremy Shales, after imposing a fifteen-second warning, gave Connors a Code of Conduct warning for "delay of game." Connors then was penalized a point when he refused to continue play. That gave Lendl the game and a 4–2 lead in the fifth set. Connors continued to protest and was given a game penalty, making it 5–2, Lendl. Supervisor Ken Farrar tried and failed to convince Connors to continue play. Instead Connors walked off the court, defaulting himself.

Connors had already pulled a forty-two-day suspension after the U.S. Open for fine accumulation. He was fined $2,500 during the Open for "using obscenity" and "verbally abusing officials" after being fined $1,500 at the Canadian Open for similar behavior. Fresh off that suspension, with his fines already standing at $5,000 going into his match with Lendl in Boca, Connors found himself facing suspension yet again.

It would have been embarrassing for Jimmy if he hadn't been able to play in his next scheduled event, the $350,000 PaineWebber Classic at the Jimmy Connors United States Tennis Center, because he had been suspended. Not only was the site in Sanibel named after him, but Connors did television commercials for PaineWebber, trading ground strokes with stockbrokers wearing three-piece suits. At the tournament's beginning, no punishment had been handed down by the Pro Council. Ironically, the decision came after Connors lost again in the semifinals, again to Lendl, and again with Jeremy Shales in the chair.

Everyone was stunned; most especially, Connors. Marshall Happer, administrator of the Pro Council, said Connors violated the provisions of the MIPTC Code of Conduct relating to the major offense of "aggravated behavior" and fined him the maximum $20,000, plus a ten weeks' suspension.

Connors considered an appeal; the suspension would keep him

from playing the French Open, but he decided against it, considering these factors instead. To a player of his wealth, $20,000 wasn't such a substantial penalty and, according to the rules, he could still play exhibitions where he could pick up five times that in a single day. In addition, he wasn't scheduled to play in any Grand Prix tournaments before the French Open anyway. If he didn't appeal, he'd only be out through the end of May. If he appealed and the appeal process dragged out and if he lost, he could miss the U.S. Open. No way was that going to happen.

The French Open survived just fine without Connors or McEnroe. Lendl won the title over Mikael Pernfors, who provided two weeks of excitement with stunning upsets over Boris Becker, Stefan Edberg, and Henri LeConte. Mac was a no-show at Wimbledon as well, and Connors made only a cameo appearance, falling in the first round to Robert Seguso. Becker defended his stunning 1985 title with a victory over Ivan Lendl.

Mac ended his vacation (and everyone else's as well) in August. Back was the deft touch and passing shots, the angry shouting and arguing with players, officials, and spectators. In his first tournament, Stratton Mountain, he entered into a war of words with Boris Becker who fought back from triple match point down to win their first confrontation in more than a year.

At the U.S. Open, Mac was eliminated in the first round by Paul Annacone. He and Peter Fleming were defaulted in the first round of doubles after arriving twenty minutes late and six minutes after the match had been forfeited. Mac was incensed that everything wasn't placed on hold pending his arrival. After all, how was the New Yorker supposed to know traffic would be so heavy on the Long Island Expressway? He made his point loud and clear. For his "verbal abuse," he was fined $4,000. He and Fleming had already been fined $1,000 each for their failure to appear.

Almost as stunning as McEnroe's ouster in the first round of both singles and doubles was Connors's ouster in the third round at the hands of Todd Witsken. North Carolina's Tim Wilkison upset Yannick Noah to become the only American to reach the quarterfinals. He became virtually a folk hero. His sprawling, diving style had already earned him the nickname "Dr. Dirt." When he lost to Stefan Edberg, for the first time in as far back as the memory bank in my head will go, there was no American among the final four left standing in the U.S. Open. Ivan Lendl successfully defended the title he had won in 1985 by defeating the big cat, Miloslav Mecir.

In Los Angeles, McEnroe gained his first tournament victory since his return from sabbatical. The tournament was even more notable for Mac's semifinal encounter with Brad Gilbert, since Brad had sent him on his way at the Masters. These two were well on the way to being very unfriendly. Tied, 3–3, in the final set, Gilbert hit a backhand passing shot down the line to go up, 30–0. The ball clearly landed in. Mac, of course, thought it clearly landed out and clearly stated his opinion in a fifteen-minute argument.

Somebody in the stands stated their opinion clearly, and Mac split his screaming between the umpire and the fan. Then a fight broke out in the stands when everyone was growing impatient and security had to be called in. By the time play continued, Gilbert didn't win another point. Does anyone still wonder why John continued to pull this stuff? Seriously.

In San Francisco he continued that winning feeling by defeating Connors in the final and the two left court with their arms wrapped around each other like old friends. Welcome back, buddy.

Even with six months off, predictably Mac finished the year suspended. He lost in the Paris Indoor to Sergio Casal (ranked 100) and lost his temper. To umpire Jeremy Shales: "You are the worst umpire I've seen in my life." Another $3,000 fine, another suspension.

In March 1987, a little more than four months later, Jeremy Shales was fired from his cushy $25,000 a year job. Shales learned of his dismissal at the end of the Lipton tournament in Key Biscayne. In that same tournament just a few days before, Mac drew the fines for his outburst in the doubles match against me and Ivan Lendl. The year was beginning in typical fashion for him and would be a record-breaker.

During the WCT Finals in Dallas, McEnroe was struggling in his match against Miloslav Mecir and didn't like the calls of umpire Gerry Armstrong. McEnroe let Armstrong and everyone sitting courtside know of his displeasure in typical bad boy fashion. Mac was given a slap on the wrist; a $2,000 fine, 2 percent of the $100,000 he earned for being runner-up in the event and .1 percent of the $2 mil he had made in endorsements in 1986. Mats Wilander, the complete opposite of McEnroe in court deportment, was fined $5,000. His transgression? Mats failed to show for a pretournament press conference to hype the WCT Finals.

AUTHOR'S NOTE: In 2003 world number-one Leyton Hewitt was fined $100,000 for failing to provide an onscreen interview to promote an ATP event. The appeal is still pending.

Later in May while practicing in Dusseldorf with his U.S. teammates in the World Team Cup, McEnroe bet his friend Gary Donnelly $100 "between now and the end of Wimbledon I won't get fined once." Four days later, he lost that bet.

Under a chorus of boos and whistles, Mac stormed off the court during a match again against Mecir, helping Czechoslovakia win the World Team Cup over the American team. He was trailing Mecir 5–7/6–2/1–2 and had raged with Rich Kaufman (the same umpire of our doubles match in Key Biscayne) against a ruling just before his departure. The emotional exit cost him $4,500 in fines: $3,000 for "leaving the court," $1,000 for "disqualification," and $500 for "unsportsmanlike conduct." Not even halfway through the year those fines put Mac over the $7,500 twelve-month limit. For that he was fined an additional $10,000. The abacus of his fine count went back to zero at that point and the count or countdown began anew. If he reached $7,500 twice in the twelve-month period, he would be subject to another $10,000 fine, plus a two-month suspension.

The abacus ran out of beads in a single match at the U.S. Open. McEnroe's third-round match against Bobo Zivojinovic stands out as possibly the worst behavior ever exhibited, not just on a tennis court but in all sports. McEnroe had taken the first set over Bobo, 6–4, but in the fourth game of the second set several of Bobo's shots had landed close to the line or right on the line and all had been called good by the linesman. This had Mac's temper close to the line or right on the line; something decidedly not good.

Serving at set point, John missed an easy forehand, a *sitter*, a shot he could have made in his sleep. With the score at deuce, Mac missed another volley and he tossed his first barb to twenty-two-year-old chair umpire Richard Ings. "Was that point important enough? It was only set point for me."

Ings had made Mac's hit list because he hadn't overruled the linesman's previous calls. Mac got the game back to deuce, but then he double-faulted and followed that with a backhand right into the net. During the changeover, Mac started up with Ings again. "Can't you see anything? That call cost me the damn set. . . . It was over, completely over, and you can't see a damn thing!"

Ings gave Mac a warning, which was Mac's cue to unleash a barrage of four-letter words all picked up by the CBS microphones courtside. Ings assessed Mac a point penalty for "obscene language."

McEnroe played the next two games of the second set without incident, but while he was changing his shirt courtside with Zivojinovic leading, 6–5, Mac began yelling at Ings again. When Ings made it clear that he had no intentions of engaging Mac in conversation, Mac turned his attention to the CBS technician holding a microphone near the net. He let loose with a string of profanities, screaming out references to oral sex and unnatural acts suggesting to the technician just what he could do with his microphone. For this he was assessed a game penalty.

McEnroe, always in control, never uttered another of his "bad words," as he so primly calls them, once he had taken Ings to the brink, thus avoiding that final straw leading to default. After winning the match, Mac actually bragged, "I'm an old pro in that situation."

Not so fast, old pro. After reviewing tapes of the incident, supervisor Ken Farrar called it "intolerable and unacceptable behavior. I can't believe I've heard a more vile disgusting attack on a chair umpire." He assessed McEnroe three different fines: $500 for the first Code of Conduct warning; $5,000 (the maximum) for cursing at Ings; and $2,000 for cursing at the CBS technician working the boom mike. One match and Mac had hit the magic $7,500 mark.

Mac appealed the fines on the grounds that they were "excessive," but the Pro Council denied his appeal. The $7,500 fine stood and for going over twice in the twelve-month period, Mac pulled an additional $10,000 debit and an automatic two-month suspension.

By reaching the round of sixteen at the Open, Mac had already made enough to cover the fines, and as for the suspension, it came at the slack time on the sanctioned schedule and the rules didn't ban participation in exhibitions. Sure, he'd have to pass up say the Swiss Indoor Championship and its winner's purse of $40,000 or the Grand Prix event in Scottsdale that paid its champion $46,000, but he could play as many exhibitions as he could fit into his schedule.

Mac's punishment had him crying all the way to the bank. In October he played the AT&T Challenge Exhibition in Atlanta. When he was awarded his winner's check of $150,000, he said, "Great way to spend a suspension!" Over the course of the sixty days, he also played exhibitions in Mexico, Florence, Antwerp, and California.

But the granddaddy of them all was the Stakes Match, tennis's answer to golf's Skins Game, where Mac was staked to $250,000 just for showing up. In the sixty days he was banned from sanctioned tennis, Mac made almost $750,000 playing exhibitions: *How I Spent My Suspension from Tennis . . .*

I'm reminded of a tiny item that appeared once in *Sports Illustrated*. Judge T. P. Poulton of Division D Circuit Court in Palm Beach County had heard that Mac might play the local tennis event, prompting him to submit "A Judge's Prayer" to the bulletin of the county bar association:

A JUDGE'S PRAYER

Dear Lord, let him come to the county. And please let him be involved in some small scrape so that he sues or is sued. And Lord, have the case fall in Division D. Finally, please Lord, have him argue after the ruling.

11:

ALONG FOR THE RIDE

IN 1982 THE UNEASY coexistence between the WCT and
the Grand Prix became open warfare. The WCT severed its ties
with the MIPTC and its Grand Prix Tour and set out on its own.
To draw players away from the more lucrative WCT Tour, the
ATP cooperated with the Pro Council and declared all twenty-
two WCT tournaments to be "special events." These were essentially exhibition tournaments which would carry no sanction and
therefore no ATP points.

The MIPTC also passed new rules which obliged most players
to commit to ten "designated" Grand Prix tournaments each year.
Those who wouldn't commit to these terms would not officially
qualify for the Grand Prix Tour and would (each week) have to go
through the qualifying rounds to gain entry into any Grand Prix
tournament.

Bjorn Borg refused to commit to ten tournaments. If he
wanted to compete on the tour, he would be relegated to the qualifying rounds. Coming off his defeats at the hands of McEnroe in
1982, he was less than enthusiastic about this, but felt obligated
to the tournament in Monte Carlo. After all, he was a resident

there to avoid income taxes and his friend Guillermo Vilas had dated Princess Caroline.

The resident of Monte Carlo decided to play in the qualies (qualifying rounds) at the Monte Carlo Country Club, and it was a box-office bonanza. There had always been qualifying rounds for the tournament, of course, but the matches played on Saturday and Sunday prior to the main event generally prompted little or no interest. With the announcement that Bjorn Borg would play, the opening round attracted two hundred journalists and several dozen photographers.

Borg's opponent in the first round of the qualies was Italian Paolo Bertolucci. Bertolucci had logged some good results over the course of his eight-year career, winning tournaments in Hamburg, Florence, Berlin, and Barcelona, but the twenty-eight-year-old playing in the qualifying rounds in Monte Carlo had never known such media attention. It literally made him a star overnight, at least for fifteen minutes. Suddenly he was thrust into the spotlight, giving interviews and being followed by photographers.

Bertolucci was happy to play Borg. Earlier in the week he had made a dinner bet with several friends, predicting that he'd wind up playing Borg in the qualies. On receiving the news, Paolo quipped that "at least I won't lose to some unknown guy." He did lose, 7–5, 6–0, the first of three qualifiers Borg would reduce to smoky rubble.

In the second round of the qualies, Borg totally annihilated Marco Ostoja of Croatia, 6–0, 6–0. In the third round, Pablo Arraya fared little better, falling 6–3, 6–1. The qualifying rounds had been a mere formality, but Borg had participated in one of the ugliest political battles to be fought in tennis since the open era. It wasn't even his battle, though, as the issue was one of power. Businessmen were fighting over who would control the sport and Borg got lost in the shuffle. In the quarterfinals of the tournament, he lost to Yannick Noah.

After playing in Monte Carlo, his only tournament of the year,

Borg was still ranked number four in the world, but he had had enough. Even though he was the defending champion at Roland Garros, he would be required to go through the qualifying rounds. He announced that he intended to pass. Prior to the event, he was approached by Phillipe Chatrier, president of the French Federation du Tenis and head of the MIPTC. Chatrier wondered why Borg wouldn't consider playing the qualifying event.

Bjorn declined to even address the insanity of the question. Chatrier was so caught up in his quest for political status (he eventually campaigned his way onto the International Olympic Committee) that he apparently missed the fact that he was asking the six-time French Open champion to *qualify* for the event!

Borg's response: "Because I don't like you."

Bjorn's nonappearance was the story of the tournament—until its end. Mats Wilander, who had taken the junior title at the French Open in 1981, became the first player since Ken Rosewall to follow a junior title with the Open championship the next year. He was also the first unseeded French Open champion in over thirty years. And the youngest champion of a Grand Slam event in the history of tennis. Borg had first won the French Open at the age of seventeen; Wilander beat that by forty-eight days.

At the press conference afterward, an American journalist asked Wilander, "Since a lot of us don't know you, please tell us something about yourself."

Wilander replied, "I think you know me now."

Ranked as the world's second-best junior behind Californian Matt Anger, no one in tennis expected him to become one of the top dozen players in the world in such a short time. Mats changed everyone's minds very quickly. On his way to capturing the French Open title, Wilander calmly and methodically knocked off four of the world's top ten players: Ivan Lendl, Vitas Gerulaitis, Jose-Luis Clerc, and, in the final, Guillermo Vilas. Along the way, Wilander stunned everyone at Stade Roland Garros by refusing to accept a bad call on match point against Clerc that would have awarded him the match.

Mats went on that year to win the Swedish Open, Geneva, and Barcelona and reached the fourth round at Wimbledon and the U.S. Open. A shoo-in for rookie of the year, Wilander became the subject of constant media attention and endless comparisons with one of history's greatest players: his countryman, Bjorn Borg.

Borg didn't defend his title at the French Open, and he didn't play Wimbledon. If the five-time Wimbledon champion and last year's finalist wished to play Wimbledon, he would have to qualify. He responded that he wasn't interested. The All England Club made several overtures to Borg, even promising that special accommodations would be made so that Borg wouldn't have to compete with everyone else at Roehampton. They never got it. They too were lost in their political ambitions and tennis fans around the world were the losers.

There were, however, a myriad of players for whom the qualifying rounds represented an opportunity to get out of the minor leagues of the satellite circuit and make it to the big time. There was always the chance to repeat John McEnroe's legendary feat in 1977, advancing all the way through the qualies at Roehampton to reach the semifinals at Wimbledon—it could happen.

Marty Davis, ranked number 104 in the world, just barely qualified for direct entry into the 128-man field at Wimbledon and a first-round bout with Mark Edmondson. Edmondson, a former Australian Open champion, was ranked twenty-fourth in the world and was the tournament's twelfth seed. Davis escaped the dangers of Roehampton, but he couldn't afford to stay in the tournament's official hotel, the Gloucester, at £70 a night and you certainly wouldn't find him bunking near Jimmy Connors at the even pricier Inn on the Park.

To afford to participate in Wimbledon, Davis split the cost of a $150 a week tiny row house with his doubles partner, Chris Dunk, and George Hardie. Dunk, ranked number 170, and Hardie, ranked number 381, were Roehampton bound.

The USTA proudly markets the U.S. Open as the "toughest tennis tournament in the world." They're wrong. By far the most tortuous experience, all things considered, is Roehampton. The qualifying tournament at the Bank of England Club in Roehampton, England, about an hour south of London, does not even remotely resemble the main event at Wimbledon. On the Monday morning preceding the main tournament, several hundred players show up hoping to qualify for the qualifying. There are no courtesy cars, no locker rooms, no players lounges. There are barely tennis courts. To be sure, there are lots of them, but the playing surface more closely resembles the cricket pitch next door.

The "good" courts near the closed clubhouse were fairly decent when they were dry, but England being England, it rained and rained and rained some more. The courts isolated at the far end of the cricket pitch are like bumpy cow pastures and the lines weave as if laid by someone having one too many nips of Beefeater gin.

In 1982 the clubhouse was closed for repairs, so the players stowed their gear and prepared their psyches in a gymnasium with folding tables and chairs. Players had to check in at 9:30 A.M., but the first round of matches didn't begin until 12:30 P.M. Some players had to wait as long as nine hours for their match.

There are no ballboys, so players chase their own balls. Sometimes there aren't even chairs to sit on during changeovers. Wimbledon's traditional supply of Robinson's Lemon Barely Water, so neatly placed on the umpire's stand, was absent on changeovers as well. By the way, I don't know of a single player who ever drank a drop of that stuff, but it's been there forever.

Players made do with pitchers of tap water. Also, the Bank of England Club sits below the landing pattern for Heathrow Airport, so there were frequent visits from low-flying planes.

George Hardie didn't make it through the three qualifying rounds at Roehampton. At twenty-eight he decided it was his last shot at Wimbledon. The former NCAA finalist called it quits and became a sports writer. Chris Dunk did make it. Drew Gitlin made it also, as did Vijay Amritraj. *Vijay Amritraj?*

Borg wouldn't play the qualies, but Vijay did. A former top ten player now ranked number thirty, Amritraj was the lone player to commit himself exclusively to the WCT and had done so with the full understanding that he would have to qualify for any Grand Prix tournament he cared to enter. He cared to enter Wimbledon.

The 1981 quarterfinalist lost in the third round to Roscoe Tanner. Because the Pro Council denied ranking points for WCT tournament results, the ranking of one of the most famous players in the world for a decade plummeted to a year-end number 382.

Native Californian Drew Gitlin reached the third round and lost also, but he was the only player in the entire tournament to give Jimmy Connors any difficulties until Connors reached Mac in the final. Gitlin was buried deep in the memory banks of the ATP computer, but with his defeat of Thierry Tulasne on a field court in front of about a dozen spectators, he earned a shot at Connors on a show court: Court One.

Connors overwhelmed Gitlin in the first set, but then Gitlin set aside who and where he was playing and started giving Connors a thing or two to think about: his strong serve and his tricky off-speed groundstrokes. Gitlin took the second set in a tiebreak.

When Connors eked out the third set, 7–5, it was 9:00 P.M. The temperature had plummeted into the low fifties and dark was just starting to settle in. Matches had been called for the night on the field courts, but Connors wanted to continue. Gitlin agreed. (What choice did he have?)

Even though Gitlin lost the fourth and deciding set, 7–5, he emerged the winner in the minds of many of the fans. Girls begged for his autograph, passersby shook his hand, and his computer ranking broke 100. Gitlin managed to put it all in perspective with the comment: "I still have to take out the garbage when I go home."

John McEnroe had a little problem with the distinction between number one and only one; while his claim to the number-one ranking was legitimate, inarguably there were many fine players of our era who had earned the right to be exactly where they were—even if that meant sharing his exalted space. Borg was gone, and it was a great loss to the sport as a whole, but while Mac myopically searched for another worthy opponent, he failed to search that quadrant over his shoulder. There was a huge field of worthy opponents sneaking up behind him. Even the era's journeymen had occasional moments of brilliance and an impact on tennis history.

Mac's 1977 run from Roehampton to the semifinals of Wimbledon pales in comparison to Mark Edmondson's run at the Australian Open in 1976. In October 1975 Mark Edmondson was a self-confessed tennis bum, working as a janitor-handyman in his hometown of Gosford, Australia, about sixty miles north of Sydney. His tennis career was less than notable. He had been defeated in the first round of the Australian Open in 1975 by John Alexander, then bounced through the British circuit, managing only a doubles title in the Rothman's tournament at Sutton. He qualified for the main draw at Wimbledon, won about $500, and returned home.

Mark entered the Australian Open in 1976 ranked number 212 in the world. At tournament's end, he was the longest longshot winner ever, not just in the revered history of the Australian Open but in any Grand Slam tournament. After having eliminated Dick Crealy and Phil Dent, Edmondson sent shock waves rippling with his semifinals victory over four-time champion and the tournament's number-one seed Ken Rosewall.

In the final, he slammed ten service aces against defending champion John Newcombe, despite gale-force winds and 130-degree heat on the stadium court at Kooyong Stadium.

The Australian Open was played for generations at Kooyong before moving to Flinders Park near downtown. One of the more interesting characteristics of Kooyong's center court is that, for drainage, the court slopes toward the back of the court at each end. The surface at the net is effectively six inches higher than each baseline, thus nullifying the advantage of a hard, flat serve.

John Newcombe was unable to handle the effective play of his younger opponent and a new Australian hero was born.

At the trophy presentation, the euphoric but nervous twenty-two-year-old Edmondson dropped the big silver bowl inscribed with names like Laver, Emerson, Hoad, and Newcombe. To this day, Mark is the lowest-ranked player ever to win a Grand Slam event and the last fellow from down under to win the Australian.

Falling in love could mean almost certain ruin for a tennis game. When both partners are professional players, it is doubly so, but Brian Teacher and Kathy May seemed to be the exception. Tennis had always been a part of their lives and their relationship. They met as ten-year-olds, playing the California junior circuit, had their first date at sixteen during a national junior tournament, then went steady right up to the time they were married.

It's not easy maintaining a marriage and one tennis career, much less two tennis careers under one roof. They carefully planned their schedules so that they were never separated for more than two weeks at a time and filled in the gaps with twice-a-day phone calls and the occasional three thousand mile plane trip just to have dinner together.

When Brian arrived in Melbourne for the Australian Open in December 1980, he was ranked twelfth in the world and seeded eighth in the tournament. Before the tournament began, Brian got a call from Kathy. He expected it to be like any other call—wishing him luck and sending her love. Instead Kathy told him she was filing for divorce.

Brian was stunned, shaken, distraught. He contemplated flying home immediately. He made flight reservations. He thought some more and eventually decided to stay in Melbourne and play the tournament instead. Coming from some dark place known to very few people, he defeated Australian Paul McNamee in the quarterfinals. He defeated Australian Peter McNamara in the semifinals. In the final he faced yet another Australian, Kim Warwick, who had defeated me in the quarterfinals and Guillermo Vilas in the semifinals. The Sydney native had the support of a very partisan rowdy Australian crowd, but Teacher won the day and, on that day, the Australian Open. Winning a Grand Slam tournament at all is a great achievement. Winning it while your personal life is falling apart is nothing short of extraordinary.

The story of the back-to-back Australian Open champion in 1981 and 1982 is remarkable as well. Johan Kriek had grown up practicing alone, thwacking balls against the wall of the screened-in veranda of his family's farmhouse—a sugarcane farm in the small South African town of Pongola; not exactly a tennis breeding ground. Tennis was a sport primarily reserved for the English-speaking population of the big cities like Cape Town and Pretoria, not for an Afrikaner like Kriek. Rugby was more his sport. He grew up with the physique of a rugged rugby player: five-foot eight, 155 pounds. When Kriek was thirteen, he passed on a promising career in rugby and moved four hundred miles from home to a public boarding school in Pretoria so he could have the benefits of a well-run tennis program. Despite this attempt to gain more opportunities to advance in tennis, Kriek came up against a wall he couldn't beat: the South African Tennis Federation.

Johan ranked in the top three in the country in each age group as a junior, yet he was once again passed over as a selection for the Federation-sponsored traveling squad because he was Afrikaan. The kids selected for the squad to travel, all expenses paid, to tournaments were English. Disillusioned by this blatant case of bigotry, Kriek followed his high school coach to Austria, where his coach had accepted work. South African newspapers blasted Kriek for "deserting" his country and, for all intents and purposes, it became next to impossible for him to ever return home.

For three years in Austria, Johan cultivated his game. It was a game centered around a blazing speed. He then ventured onto the satellite circuit. In 1978 Kriek came to the United States to play Florida's W.A.T.C.H. satellite circuit.

W.A.T.C.H., the World Association of Tennis Champions, was formed by two ranked U.S. players, Larry Turville and Armistead

Neely, in February 1971. The two players had the dubious distinction of being rejected by Lamar Hunt's WCT Tour *and* Bill Riordan's independent indoor circuit. With about fifty other idle pros, they formed a seven-week tour with total prize money of about $15,000.

There were satellite circuits just about everywhere there was tennis, but by 1978, W.A.T.C.H. had evolved into the country's largest breeding ground for aspiring tennis pros. Every weekend, 250 players tried to qualify for eight open spots in the thirty-two-player fields for that week's tournament. These were youngsters trying to get a foothold in the world of professional tennis. At the end of the seven-week tour, the top sixteen players on the circuit played in a "masters" final and were awarded points by the ATP. The lead players might even earn enough points to play qualifying events in the big leagues. The odds were enormous against any one individual emerging from the pack.

Kriek was no stranger to long odds. He also believed in that great underlying principle of meritocracy: Win enough and eventually you get ranked high enough to play anywhere. He emerged big time. He won one of the events, then reached the semifinals in two others and the quarterfinals in another. By the U.S. Open, Johan's ranking was high enough to get him straight in to the event. He went all the way to the quarterfinals before losing to Vitas Gerulaitis.

By the end of the year, Kriek's ranking had jumped 251 notches to number twenty-seven in the world. He had made it, but that's when he learned a lesson I picked up from Ivan Lendl: You cannot reach a certain level and expect to just stay there. Staying there was another challenge.

Kriek joined forces with Hank Jungle, a retired U.S. Air Force colonel who worked with the Gullikson twins, Terry Moor, and Mike Cahill, and who happened to be a pretty good player himself. Jungle had seen Kriek on the tour and knew his strengths (incredible speed, athleticism, and aggressiveness) and his weaknesses (a vulnerable forehand, a lack of a kick serve, and his biggest handicap, lousy footwork on soft courts—on grass his dazzling speed landed him right on his butt).

Kriek tended to steer his forehand under pressure and to always go down the line with it. Jungle saw this; opponents saw it and exploited it. Johan had never learned a topspin serve, and not that there's ever a good time to double fault, but it always seemed to happen to Johan at the worst possible times. Kriek and Jungle worked tirelessly on the forehand and the serve and those problems were easily solved simply with more and more practice. Just before Wimbledon 1981, Jungle started working on Kriek's footwork on grass, using dead tennis balls to force the speedster to hit a shot and recover immediately.

The results speak for themselves. At the Bristol warm-up event, Kriek reached the semifinals, losing to the eventual winner, Mark Edmondson. At Wimbledon itself, he made it to the quarterfinals, bowing to eventual champ McEnroe, then Kriek took two consecutive grass court titles: Newport and the Australian Open, defeating Steve Denton, my fellow Texan, in the finals. Johan successfully defended his Australian Open title the next year. He wasn't falling on his butt on grass anymore, and the kid from an isolated corner of the world who had gotten no support from his own Federation was in the top ten of all tennis players in the world.

When Johan defended his title in Melbourne in 1982, his opponent in the final was that same Texan, the guy who once punched out McEnroe, as you may recall: Steve Denton.

The University of Texas had three All-Americans in tennis in 1978: Kevin Curren, Gary Plock, and Steve Denton. The small Texas town where Denton was raised, Driscoll, population 638, had one very decrepit tennis court, so Denton's mother would drive him to Corpus Christi fifty miles away to learn the game. Basketball was more accessible. Denton had been a standout in high school basketball and was offered scholarships, but Denton thought he was too slow to have a future in basketball and decided to gamble on a future in tennis instead. Coach Dave Snyder took a gamble, signing him to play college tennis. It was a gamble that paid off. During his time with the Longhorns, Denton accumulated an 85–22 singles record and a 72–18 doubles record.

Curren and doubles partner Gary Plock had huge success in the 1978 NCAA tournament, defeating the nation's number-one duo of Stanford's John McEnroe and Bill Maze. As it happens, McEnroe and Maze played each other in a singles match immediately preceding their doubles match against Curren and Plock. McEnroe being McEnroe, he got into a war of words with Maze. They had never been beaten as a pair, but the bickering carried over into the doubles match and they were easy pickings for Curren and Plock. Curren and Plock reached the finals, but fell to UCLA's John Austin and Bruce Nichols.

Unlike Johan Kriek, Kevin Curren got strong support from South Africa's tennis association and was South Africa's junior champion in 1976, but because South Africa offered no development programs after the junior years, Curren too headed for the United States. He had been offered scholarships from many U.S. colleges, but sight unseen he came to the University of Texas, largely on the advice of fellow South African Cliff Drysdale, who lived for a time in Austin and was familiar with Dave Snyder. Drysdale reviewed the list of schools offering scholarships to Curren and recommended the University of Texas.

Curren won the NCAA singles title in 1979, upsetting Trinity's Erick Iskersky. This was a particularly satisfying win as Iskersky had defeated Curren three times over the course of the season. Iskersky and partner Ben McKown pulled out the doubles title.

Plock had exhausted his eligibility, but Curren and Denton returned to UT in 1979, became roommates, and formed a duo that a year later began to wreak havoc on the pro community. In their first pro doubles tournament together in Richmond in 1980, Curren and Denton nearly reached the semifinals, losing in the quarterfinals to Victor Amaya and Hank Pfister, 12–10, in a third-set tiebreaker. The following week they notched their first doubles title in Denver, defeating Wojtek Fibak and Heinz Gunthardt. By the end of the year, Curren and Denton had added a title in Basel, a runner-up finish in Washington, D.C., a runner-up finish in South Orange, a semifinal showing, and three quarterfinal results, the sum of which qualified them for the Masters.

In 1981 Curren and Denton set out to prove their initial success wasn't a fluke. They emerged from their sophomore year as pros with the titles in Monterrey, the U.S. Clay Court Championship in Indianapolis, and the Stockholm Open, as well as runner-up finishes at the Belgian Indoor and Queen's Club. Curren and Denton advanced to the quarterfinals or better in thirteen of the twenty-two events they had entered and once again they qualified for the Masters. They were the number-two-ranked doubles team in the world behind Fleming and McEnroe. Curren and Denton reached the championship round of the Masters, losing to Fleming and McEnroe.

There was nothing complicated about their method of attack on a tennis court. They didn't fool around with drinks or finesse shots; they relied on raw power. Their most powerful weapon was Denton's first serve, prefaced by a twisting, foot-sliding motion that resembles a charging bull (earning him the nickname among fellow pros of "the Bull" although the sobriquet could also apply to his alma mater, the Texas Longhorns; his stocky build; or even more likely to the content of the stories he was prone to telling), and was a bullet fired with such velocity that opponents were left swinging at a yellow blur. (In 1984 Steve Denton broke the world record for fastest serve at 138 miles an hour, a record that stood for thirteen and a half years until Greg Rusedski fired a shot at 149 miles per hour at Indian Wells in 1998.)

Despite his great success in doubles and despite that killer serve, Denton was a perennial first-round loser in singles and his ranking was deep in the 400s. Hardly anyone in the top hundred worried when they saw his name on the draw sheet. That was destined to change however, when Curren and Denton became "Warren's Boys," hiring Australian Davis Cupper Warren Jacques (then living in Dallas) to help them out as their coach. For Steve Denton in particular, Jacques managed a complete overhaul of the player's life.

The main problem with Steve in Jacques's estimation was that the six-foot-two Denton was overweight by at least thirty pounds. Jacques ran Steve's tail off for months and months until he achieved his objective, making Denton a lean, mean fighting machine.

The pounds dropped, and Steve's ranking rose exponentially to number 150 by late 1981. It didn't stop there. Denton startled everyone in the tennis world by reaching the semifinals in Johannesburg and in Sydney. He was seriously unlike any prototypical tennis pro, clunky and awkward, and that serve. . . . It was no fluke, though, when he reached the finals of the Australian Open. Unseeded, Steve used his serve to overpower higher-ranked players day after day, losing to Kriek in four sets, but not before extending him to two tiebreakers and saving seven match points. As Kriek pointed out after the match, "It's incredible for a guy to come back and win seven match points. . . . It shows he's not just a great doubles player."

His showing at the Australian Open in 1981 set the stage for Denton's big surge in 1982. Jacques was confident that he could get Steve into the top twenty by the end of the year. They made it by August. That was the month of his back-to-back upsets of Vitas Gerulaitis and John McEnroe to reach the final of the ATP Championship in Cincinnati.

Steve also reached the final in Metz, France, losing to Erick Iskersky. And the semifinals in Melbourne, losing to Gerulaitis; the semifinals in the Sydney Indoor, losing to McEnroe; and the quarterfinals of Las Vegas, Toronto, Tokyo, Frankfurt, and Columbus.

Curren and Denton captured the U.S. Open doubles championship and Denton ended the year again by reaching the final of the Australian Open, where he again lost to Johan Kriek. *Tennis*

Magazine named Denton the most improved player in 1982, and under the tutelage and gruel-age of Warren Jacques, his ranking had moved up to number thirteen in the world in singles, and he qualified for the Volvo Masters in singles and doubles.

Warren Jacques missed his true calling; he should have been a drill sergeant. I say that honestly, but affectionately. In 1983 I traveled informally with Warren and Kevin and Steve and had my best year ever. Jacques has a way of extracting the best from his players while making the whole training process a little more fun.

In the spring Curren contracted Rocky Mountain spotted fever. Despite the ensuing sometimes overwhelming fatigue, Kevin reached the finals in Milan, defeating Paul McNamee and Guillermo Vilas and knocking me out in the semifinals before losing to Ivan Lendl.

Wimbledon 1983 is etched permanently in my memory for what it meant to me personally, but it was a memorable occasion for many players for many reasons. It was the year that saw Borg's return to Wimbledon, not with a Donnay racket but with an NBC badge. Regardless of who won the title in singles or doubles, Wimbledon 1983 was the year of the Wimbledon journeyman.

To fully appreciate Wimbledon is to appreciate some long-standing (if absolutely senseless) traditions. As I write this, I am saddened by the fact that some of these have gone by the wayside in just the last ten years or so. As goofy as some of them are, I came to look forward to navigating their course each year.

The first noticeable difference a player discovers on arrival at Wimbledon is that practice on the actual tournament courts is almost nonexistent. Main draw players are allowed to book one half-hour on a field court during the week before the event. Not one half-hour per day. One for the week. You can have all the time you want at Aorangi Park, but the tournament courts are special. Seeded players get half an hour each day. Practice hard. Past Wimbledon singles champions are honorary members of the All England Club and (as members) can play as much as they want. Keep practicing.

Another great Wimbledon tradition is that nobody practices on Centre Court. Ever. The court is used during the fortnight of Wimbledon and for Davis Cup ties only with one exception. One week prior to the championships each year one foursome of club members (not Borg, Connors, McEnroe, or Becker) are invited to play a couple of sets of doubles to "break in" the court. It has absolutely no effect on the playing surface, but it is a tradition.

The first Monday at Wimbledon every year is unquestionably the best day of tennis on the calendar. Every male player in the game is scheduled for play without exception (apart from legitimate injuries). There are no "Wednesday starts" for the superstars. There are no preferential tee times. If you wish to see men's tennis and you have only one day to do it, this is your ticket. At 2:00 P.M. sharp the defending champion has the honor of opening the championships and that match will be followed by matches the tournament committee feels are "Centre Court worthy."

In 1983 the tournament committee deemed the match between former champion Stan Smith and Trey Waltke to be "Centre Court worthy." In retrospect, it was a great five-setter and also significant in that Trey on that day completed his personal "Stan Slam." He now had defeated Smith on every court surface—hard, grass, clay, and indoors. What the Wimbledon committee could not have expected was Trey's sense of style. Ray Moore affectionately bestowed the nickname "Westwood Willie" on Trey Waltke because he epitomized the relaxed lifestyle of his Los Angeles neighborhood. Trey was very much a free spirit, and no one but him could have pulled off what he did with such panache.

Trey appeared on Centre Court that Monday sporting an outfit the likes of which the All England Club hadn't seen in many decades: traditional white long flannel pants and white button-down long-sleeved shirt—and an ATP necktie for a belt. No journeyman that I can remember ever stole the headlines so effectively. Waltke's five-set victory over Smith advanced him to the second round, where he was eliminated by Lendl, but he was the talk of the tournament. Trey got the idea looking at old pictures of tennis and expected he'd get quite a laugh (which he did), but he didn't expect something else he got—a clothing endorsement contract.

Steve Denton, Kevin Curren, and I (traveling together under the watchful eye of Warren Jacques) all came into Wimbledon with high hopes. The three of us journeymen were seeded ninth, twelfth, and fourteenth respectively.

Certainly nothing can erase the memory of Curren's win over the tournament favorite and defending champ, Jimmy Connors. The match took place on Court Two, "the Graveyard." Connors had reached at least the quarterfinals of Wimbledon every year since 1972, but he wouldn't reach them in 1983. Curren beat Connors in four sets that included two tiebreaks: 6–3, 6–7, 6–3, 7–6. Curren, who had yet to lose his serve during four rounds in the event, buried Connors with an astounding thirty-three aces!

My path to the round of sixteen was mostly uneventful and ended there with my three-hour, three-set marathon against McEnroe.

Steve Denton, the highest seed of the three of us at number nine, was upset in the first round of the tournament by Chris Lewis in five sets. Lewis then steamrolled his way to a semifinal confrontation with twelfth-seeded Curren.

Chris Lewis spent an enormous amount of effort and time trying to stay on the ground. After being on three different airplanes that were forced to make emergency landings, Lewis developed a very healthy phobia about flying that proved problematic in the nomadic world of professional tennis. To get around the problem, Lewis kept cars in Europe and North America so that he could limit his flying to the absolute minimum.

Lewis had a reckless style of play, and his most formidable weapons were his stamina and his quickness. One of the hardest workers and most fit players in the pro game, Lewis did intensive drills during his on-court training and was an avid runner, both of sprints and long distance. Paul McNamee once described

Lewis's running habits as "You wouldn't drive your car that far." Chris also took up karate to improve his reflexes and quickness.

Ranked number 91, the native of Auckland, New Zealand, had only earned $34,000 going into Wimbledon. One London newspaper dubbed him "Mr. Nobody." By the end of the fortnight, Chris Lewis was definitely somebody. Lewis staged a remarkable comeback in the semis against Curren, down 0–3 in the fifth set. The match redefined *marathon*, and it was the long-distance runner Lewis who finished first. No matter what Curren dished out, Lewis took it in stride, scrambling all over the court, lunging and diving and returning seemingly impossible shots to win, 6–7, 6–4, 7–6, 6–7, 8–6.

Suddenly "Mr. Nobody" was a household name when he became only the seventh unseeded player in Wimbledon history to reach the finals of Wimbledon. He was unseeded and the first New Zealander to play for the title since Tony Wilding in 1914. With the win over Curren and a berth in the finals, Lewis received over a thousand telegrams from well-wishers and was flooded with so much supportive mail they had to give him an extra locker just to hold it all. Lewis went into the finals at Wimbledon with the only attitude he could: "Just give it everything you've got." He didn't have enough. He lost to John McEnroe, 6–2, 6–2, 6–2.

Tim and Tom Gullikson were identical twins. Both sported the same thick mop of curly black hair, the same stocky five-foot-eleven frame—identical, but Tim and Tom Gullikson were mirror twins. That made for one sure fire way of telling them apart. Tim was right-handed and Tom was left-handed. This oddity should have ended all confusion, but in one instance it created more.

It might be wise even all these long years later not to mention the name Gullikson to German player Karl Meiler. He lost a match in 1977 to T. Gullikson in San Jose, 6–3, 3–6, 6–2, and thought not much about the loss. Meiler knew that Gullikson was an up-and-coming young player from America, but that was about all he knew—just a loss to a newcomer he didn't really know anything about. A couple of weeks later, Karl faced T. Gullikson again in Memphis and lost again, 6–2, 6–3.

This loss almost gave him a complete nervous breakdown. Meiler never realized they were two separate players. He had played Tim first and then Tom, and in the locker room Karl wailed and babbled about retiring: The tour now had a player who could beat him right-handed one week and left-handed the next. It was just too much to bear.

Eventually, someone let Meiler in on the Gulliksons' secret, and Karl stuck with the tour awhile longer, but it's a good thing he didn't last until 1985, when "Dual Hand Luke" Jensen was just joining the tour. Luke was equally adept at serving right-handed or left-handed and constantly confounded opponents by switching at will.

When the Gullikson twins were children, the boys would wake to the magical sound of a tennis ball leaving a racket. The courts of La Crosse State University were across the street, just outside their bedroom window, and the boys were at the courts so often that they became unofficial mascots. They never played a national junior tournament but starred on the college tennis team at Northern Illinois University.

Perhaps the best shots of Tom Gullikson's life came in a doubles match when he wasn't paired with his brother—a once-in-a-lifetime opportunity. In 1976 there was a small tennis exhibition in Rockford, Illinois, featuring Rod Laver and Roy Emerson. A player named Dick Johnson asked Tom if he'd pair with him in doubles against the legends. Of course Tom couldn't say yes fast enough. On his first serve, Tom blasted an ace past Emerson and Laver. On match point, he hit a topspin lob over Emerson's head.

In the locker room afterward, the Aussies shook the kid's hand and then went out to play singles, leaving him alone—with Laver's sports bag. Who could resist sneaking a peek at what secrets might lie behind the great one's success? To hear Tom tell it, there were no secrets. Apparently the guy was just really good at the game.

That was the first time Tom entertained the thought of becoming a professional—and why not. When they did join the tour, they came upon good results gradually. Tom came up with a few good results in that first year, but it was Tim who had more success out of the gate. He was named the ATP Newcomer of the Year in 1977.

They did everything together. On one Monday morning in 1981, they even held the same spot on the computer rankings: tied number forty-four. Though each would play very well in singles, their greatest success as pros, not surprisingly, came as a doubles team. The twins were ranked in the top ten among doubles teams, but perhaps their most impressive showing came after defeating Curren and Denton, reaching the finals at Wimbledon in 1983.

Tom was crying as they received their award from the Duke and Duchess of Kent, not because they had lost to McEnroe and Fleming, but in utter amazement at how far he and his brother had come from those boys who woke to that magical sound of tennis balls every morning. Sometimes, as Grantland Rice observed, it truly isn't about whether you win or lose, but how you play the game.

Another pair of brothers who knew how to play the game hailed from New Jersey. Sandy and Gene Mayer. Raised by the legendary Dr. Mayer (no one knows whether he was really a doctor or just a great coach), both brothers were exceptional junior players who went on to play for Dick Gould at Stanford. Sandy, the elder, set a pretty high standard, winning the NCAA Championships in 1973. He would be the first of Dick Gould's ten NCAA singles champions over a remarkable college coaching career. Barely two months later, Sandy made his first mark in the professional world by advancing to the semifinals of Wimbledon before falling to Alex Metreveli. Two years later he would team with Vitas Gerulaitis to win the Wimbledon doubles title.

To watch the two Mayer brothers one would never imagine they were raised in the same household, much less coached by the same father. Their shots, form, style, and court presence are diametrically opposed in almost every respect. Sandy looked like he fell right out of a textbook, with classic short, flat ground strokes and a straightforward serve-and-volley style. Always charging forward, Sandy had no great mysteries or nuances in his game; he just did it extremely well. Gene, on the other hand . . .

The first thing you noticed about Gene Mayer is that he hit with two hands off of both sides. Sometimes he would switch his hands from forehand to backhand, sometimes not. He also tended to play from the backcourt a lot more than his brother. When Gene did venture to the net, he would usually end the point with a delicate angle volley. It is virtually impossible to describe Gene's serve, except that it seemed disjointed somehow and had more hitches than a dog's hind leg. It carried him to a ranking of number four in the world and thirteen singles titles worldwide.

The year 1983 marked a sad note for a couple of Australian journeymen. Paul McNamee and Peter McNamara had as a team won fourteen career doubles titles, including two Wimbledon crowns. They were national heroes back home in Australia—known as "the Super Macs"—and each had earned plenty of respect in singles as well, McNamara achieving a ranking in the top ten. At Wimbledon McNamara retired, unvoluntarily.

The twenty-eight-year-old Australian won the biggest title of his career in Brussels, beating Ivan Lendl in an electrifying final that had the crowd chanting his name. The victory boosted him to number seven on the ATP computer, his highest career ranking. A week later in Rotterdam, McNamara, the third seed, was in a war of attrition with qualifier Jiri Granat. Granat had taken the first set, 7–6, and the second set went the distance as well when it happened. McNamara took a fall on the sandpaperlike surface, tearing ligaments in his knee in the first-round match. The damage was so severe that after months of attempted rehabilitation, Peter was forced to give up tennis.

McNamara had labored in obscurity for years before breaking into the big time. He had played on the satellite circuit in France, where the winner was paid in bottles of wine. Peter also made the mistake of winning a tournament on the Italian satellite circuit in Sicily. His victory over a hometown boy apparently enraged the partisan crowd to the extent that McNamara was forced to leave the court with an armed guard escort.

The Super Macs were the stylistic opposite of Curren and Denton. They had a flair for improvisation, constantly attempting difficult shots and unorthodox placements. They won three Grand Slam doubles titles, the Australian Open, and Wimbledon twice. As a duo, they gave the best doubles team ever—McEnroe and Fleming—absolute fits. They totally dismantled McEnroe and Fleming in the doubles final of Wimbledon in 1982. That match had been shortened at Mr. McEnroe's request from the traditional best-of-five sets to an abbreviated best-of-three.

The Aussies went to the press conference afterward slightly uncomfortable with the entire situation. McNamee and McNamara did manage to explain the changes to the press corps and remarked at how easy the victory had been. In typical Aussie form, they actually claimed that they would have been more comfortable with the win had it been played as originally planned.

The Super Macs had been friends since they were seven years old. They had won fourteen doubles titles together, but now Paul McNamee was on his own. Not many players were better equipped to deal with an adjustment or transition.

About four years before McNamara's knee injury, and midway through a career that was quite successful in doubles but somewhat lackluster in singles, Paul decided to give his tennis game a complete overhaul, a total transformation. In response to changing times, advancements in racket technology, and the emergence of bigger, faster, stronger players using loads of topspin, McNamee stepped away from the tour for a few months. During that time, he reinvented himself from a Ken Rosewall type with flat shots and a one-handed slice backhand using a traditional wooden racket into a Borg type with a western forehand, two-handed backhand, and a Prince oversized graphite racket.

In the spring of 1979, Paul McNamee showed up at Harry Hopman's tennis camp in Florida, not for a couple of weeks of intense conditioning or to correct a minor flaw in his game, but to learn a new backhand. To say the least, Hopman was skeptical. He felt that the quintessential journeyman might have been over-ambitious, but McNamee was persistent and eventually won over the great old coach.

For four months, McNamee spent eight hours a day working on the backhand. It was exhausting and at times heartbreaking, but Paul's attitude never wavered. He was the epitome of perseverance, and all the hard work paid off big-time when he and his new two-handed backhand rejoined the tour in early 1980. Rarely have players been so surprised by anything as they were to see Paul playing a totally unfamiliar style—and winning.

At the U.S. Open, McNamee lost a five-set match to John Lloyd that could barely have been any tighter: 5–7, 6–7, 7–5, 7–6, 7–6. Paul reached the semifinals of two Grand Prix tournaments—Santiago and Bogotá—and in doubles, he and McNamara won five Grand Prix titles, including the Australian Open. In 1980 Paul won his first singles title in Palm Harbor, defeating the great Stan Smith. McNamee teamed with Paul Kronk to take the doubles title there as well. With McNamara, Paul took the doubles title in Houston and at the WCT Finals in Dallas. At the WCT Tournament of Champions at Forest Hills, McNamee and McNamara reached the doubles finals, bowing to Fleming and McEnroe in three tough sets. Harry Hopman was proudest of anybody as he observed Paul winning with shots learned only months ago and with mountains of determination.

At the French Open, Paul McNamee's new style paid big dividends. His confidence soared on the red clay, using Borg-style topspin forehands and two-handed backhands. Paul earned the title of "Mr. Tiebreaker" when he took down John McEnroe in the third round, 7–6, 6–7, 7–6, 7–6. The match was unbelievably tense throughout, but McNamee not only didn't show any fear, he was practically a ham throughout (which, of course, irritated Mac to no end), turning to the crowd at the most critical times with a huge grin.

Following his win over McEnroe, McNamee faced Wojtek Fibak in the fourth round. After dropping the first two sets, McNamee fought off three match points and took the third set in (what else?) a tiebreak. By the time Fibak served for the match at 5–3 in the fourth, the leader seemed to be on his last legs. Only with his fifth match point was Fibak able to end McNamee's run.

Then came Wimbledon, where McNamee and McNamara won the doubles crown with a four-set victory over Bob Lutz and Stan Smith. Along the way they had knocked off two previous championship teams: Raul Ramirez and Brian Gottfried in the quarterfinals and Fleming and McEnroe in the semifinals. Paul McNamee had proved that all the work was worth it. The big gamble had paid off.

At the beginning of 2003, the Dalai Lama imparted these words of wisdom to the world: "When you lose, don't lose the lesson."

At the beginning of 1987, when another of the era's notable journeymen, Tim Mayotte, defeated John McEnroe to take the title at the United States Pro Indoor in Philadelphia, McEnroe remarked, "This taught me a lesson, but I'm not sure what it is."

12:

MENTAL CASES

IN 1975 I WAS A SOPHOMORE at Trinity University in San Antonio, Texas. I'd had a successful freshman year, alternating as the number-one player on our team and reaching the quarterfinals of the NCAA Championships in Corpus Christi, Texas. Billy Martin had won the title that year as a freshman, playing for UCLA. He immediately turned pro and started making his way up the ATP computer.

Because I was still eligible for junior tennis, I played the national junior circuit all summer, earning a singles ranking of number two in the United States. Not exactly keeping pace with Billy Martin, but solid nonetheless. My doubles partner, Tony Giammalva, and I won three straight tournament titles, including the Nationals at Kalamazoo. We were jointly ranked number one in the country in doubles. Naturally, as I headed back to San Antonio, I had high expectations for my sophomore year.

By the time Christmas break arrived, I had managed to work my way down to number six on my Trinity team. I still practiced just as hard and I didn't make any great changes in my shots or strategy. Somehow I just seemed to lose all the time. I didn't know what was wrong, but I did know that something had to change.

Bill Stanley would wipe the floor up with me if I ever described him as a Yoda or a guru or some Grape Nuts sort of guy, but he was my first introduction to sports psychology. Bill had been enormously successful as a salesman in the floor-finishing products industry in West Texas. In fact, he was such a great salesperson that in time he began to teach sales techniques to the sales forces of companies in a variety of industries. This eventually led to a new business: teaching motivational techniques. Bill taught about the importance of personal growth based on the power within individuals to achieve their dreams.

Over the Christmas break at the end of 1975, my dad arranged for me to meet with Bill Stanley. By then I was so frustrated with my tennis results that I was willing to try almost anything, even if I had no idea what that might turn out to be.

With no small measure of teenage sullenness, my first comment to Mr. Stanley was along the lines of "My dad says you're gonna fix my tennis." He set me straight immediately, explaining that I was the only person who could fix my tennis game—or anything else, for that matter. Not him, not my dad, just me, and it was going to take a lot of work.

Now, in 1975 there was no such industry as *sports psychology*. That was a term that would become popular several years later, along with everything else in the self-help section of the bookstores. Bill Stanley and I merely worked on all the principles that everyone takes for granted today, such as goal-setting, positive thinking, and visualization, and we developed a game plan for all the improvements I wanted to make. The first step was to define the goals and put them in writing. Somehow I left that first meeting with a piece of paper saying I was going to play number one for my Trinity tennis team and that I was going to win the NCAA's in May. Six months later.

Throughout the spring tennis season of my sophomore year, I practiced the techniques and dedicated myself to learning all the principles. It wasn't always fun and it wasn't always easy, but the results were dramatic. I managed, with Bill Stanley's help, to climb to number one on my Trinity team and stay there for the spring season.

When our team arrived in Corpus Christi for the NCAA's in May, I found that I had been seeded sixth, well behind the favorite, Peter Fleming. Peter had transferred to UCLA from Michigan and was the odds-on favorite to follow in Billy Martin's footsteps. By the end of the tournament, I had managed to beat Fleming in a four-set final to take the title and the national championship. I was a believer. My first phone call was to Bill Stanley, asking, "Where do we go from here?"

I turned pro immediately thereafter, continuing to make practice of the principles that Bill Stanley taught and by the following February had climbed to an ATP world ranking of number twenty-three.

As I traveled the pro circuit, I sensed that I wasn't the only player who had been exposed to principles similar to those I learned from Bill Stanley. The interesting thing was that nobody spoke of it and there were certainly no locker room discussions about what might or might not work effectively.

Two exceptions were Torbin Ulrich and Jeff Borowiak. They made no secret of their meditations and Eastern philosophies. They flew in the face of conventional practice sessions, opting instead for workouts at 4:00 A.M. without lights. Apparently this was supposed to heighten awareness and increase focus. The spiritual approach they adopted to developing their skills would make Michael Murphy (*Golf in the Kingdom*) proud and went way beyond the theories put forth by Timothy Gallway in *The Inner Game of Tennis*.

Most of the players would have been happy to avoid the place that Borowiak and Ulrich had found on their journeys into spiritual tennis—if for no other reason than to avoid repeating one of Ulrich's finer moments. As the story goes, Torben had just managed to win a hard-fought first-set tiebreaker from a respected opponent when he called the other player to the net for a chat. Seems that Torben felt happy with how well the match had gone so far—and how well they'd both played. He said he was satisfied that it was the best tennis of which he was capable. Fearing that things could only go downhill from there, he chose to concede the rest of the match, instead heading to the locker room to reflect on his fine play in the first set.

Even though most players avoided the subject (for fear of being labeled as "flighty"), it was apparent that many were using at least some similar techniques in order to achieve peak performance. Words and phrases were heard on the practice court and in locker rooms that seemed to indicate an awareness of common principles such as imagery, visualizations, or relaxation techniques.

Brian Teacher and Peter Fleming were early practitioners of yoga. Being from Los Angeles, they apparently had been influenced by fellow UCLA athletes, such as Kareem Abdul Jabbar and Bill Walton. They used yoga and other exercises to increase their flexibility along with their concentration skills. Brian Teacher once gave me a book called *Zen in the Art of Archery* that dealt with focus and concentration. With my earlier background in sports psychology, I found it very helpful.

It wasn't until the early '80s that sports psychology formally announced its arrival on the tennis tour. It was 1983 and Jim Loehr, a practicing psychologist, made overtures to a number of players, claiming that he could help them by teaching "the mental game." His goal was to enlist players as clients who would pay him for his teaching. Now, over a number of years, Dr. Loehr has helped lots of players and contributed greatly to the mental side of the sport. But when he first arrived on the tour he got off to a slow start. There may have been a couple of reasons for that.

First, remember that Dr. Loehr was approaching players who were already successful and, like myself, were probably already making use of mental techniques, even if they didn't advertise it.

I know I met with Jim a couple of times to hear what he had to offer, but I didn't feel inclined to tell him about Bill Stanley and the work we'd been doing for years.

Second, when Dr. Loehr first arrived on the tour, his theories were little better than Borowiak's, primarily because his approach was that of a doctor/researcher who had no hands-on experience at the professional level of our sport.

The research consisted of interviewing hundreds of great athletes, all champions in their respective sports. The same question was asked of each: "Describe for me in as much detail as possible the time when you played the absolute best tennis [or golf, or basketball, and so on] that you've ever played."

It was a logical question. Certainly we'd all like to know if there were commonalities that might exist in *peak performance*, whether in our sport or others. And we'd all like to know how that peak performance felt to the athlete who was experiencing it. Most importantly, whatever that peak performance felt like, certainly it's what we all wanted to do every time we played.

Well, you can imagine the answers that came from all the athletes:

- "Everything just flowed."
- "I was totally relaxed."
- "I wasn't thinking at all."
- "I seemed to be outside my body."
- "I felt as if I was watching myself play."

Surprise, all the athletes were describing the exact same experience. This was a breakthrough moment in sports! The researchers had found that there was a state of mind that was common to all the best performances of all the best athletes in every sport.

Of course they were describing "the zone." And their brilliant conclusion at the end of all this research was: "In order to play your best, you should zone."

This spawned a whole wave of youngsters who tried to improve their tennis by "relaxing" and "not thinking." They were hoping with all their heart to "zone" as often as possible, believing that this must be the secret to McEnroe's success. It certainly couldn't be hard practice or physical exercise, because after all he claimed to do neither.

The thought of some college kid believing for even a minute that if he only "zoned" well enough, he might be able to beat Boris Becker or Ivan Lendl . . .

To Dr. Loehr's credit, he did gradually develop his teachings on the mental side of the game to include more than "hoping to zone." In fact, he joined forces with Nick Bollettieri at Bollettieri's Academy in Bradenton to help young players with that side of the sport while they continued to hone their shot skills and train physically in the gym. The partnership was a good one and really helped a lot of kids, even the ones who never made the tour.

Along the way, numerous other sports psychology specialists joined the ranks working with players such as Jimmy Arias, Brad Gilbert, and, most notably, Ivan Lendl.

Despite defeating John McEnroe in five sets to win the French Open in 1984, Lendl had been labeled as a choker in Grand Slam events. He always did well, making the semis or finals, but he never won, and that didn't make sense for someone who was so dominating in other events. In 1984 Ivan enlisted the help of a professional psychotherapist, Dr. Alexis Castori, who had never worked with athletes before. She was confident enough in her theories, though. So much so that she was willing to make a bet with Lendl that if he worked with her, Ivan would win the U.S. Open in 1985.

Remember, Lendl had lost in the finals of the Open the last two years, first to Connors and then to McEnroe, even though his overall record against them both was far superior.

The psychologist believed that Lendl had created his own negative pressure in Grand Slam events and that he needed to *redefine* the meaning and importance of Grand Slam tournaments in order to play his best tennis. (Maybe she felt "zoning" was too much to ask.)

The psychologist vowed that if Lendl didn't win the Open after her intervention, *she* would pay *him*. Lendl took the bet, and she and Ivan teamed up to work on his focus and concentration.

Lendl's instinctive work ethic was fairly simple to grasp. First work hard, then work harder. What Dr. Castori wanted Lendl to "work" on was relaxing and letting go. He might not "zone" but he would eventually get out of his own way and stop interfering with his own abilities. She also got Lendl to practice "mental aerobics," a series of mental-focus exercises. This was easy for Ivan to accept because of the success he had seen with physical exercises. One such practice was to take a small object—a ring, a coin, a tennis ball—and describe out loud for five minutes what you saw when looking at the object. Try doing the exercise for a couple of minutes, and you'll realize just how focused you have to be to stick with it for five.

On court a spectator might see Ivan ritualistically inspecting the strings of his racket or taking sawdust from his pocket. What Ivan would "see" is where his next serve would go, where the return would go, where he'd place his next shot. What these little exercises enabled him to do was stop worrying about the outcome or the importance of the match or even the importance of the next point.

Lendl came to realize that a Grand Slam final wasn't life or death; it was only a tennis match that he could either win or lose— just like every other tennis match he played all year long. Tennis was only a game. Any pressure that existed was self-imposed.

At the 1985 U.S. Open, Lendl easily swept me aside in the second round (I'm sure he "zoned") and only dropped one set in the entire tournament on his collision course with his nemesis: the number-one seed and the number-one player in the world, John McEnroe.

Lendl made equally short work of McEnroe, winning the final is straight sets ("zoning," of course) and gaining his first of three

U.S. Open titles in a row. He replaced McEnroe at number one on the ATP computer and remained there for a remarkable 156 consecutive weeks.

He also paid off his bet with Dr. Alexis Castori.

When Ivan introduced me to Dr. Castori in 1986, I was anxious to compare her teachings with those I'd learned from Bill Stanley and what I'd gathered from Dr. Loehr. Again I purposely avoided telling her that I had done considerable work on the mental side of the game. To do so might influence her approach and I felt it was wiser to simply let her teach away. I was impressed that most of the exercises she prescribed were consistent with the other teachings. I was able to be motivated by a fresh outlook and believe she was very helpful.

By the time I met Dr. Castori, I was over thirty years old and had to be realistic about my goals. With two knee surgeries behind me, in addition to my age, it wasn't practical for me to be aiming at the top ten. But with her help and Ivan's (along with everyone else's), I was able to hang on for another three years that might not have been possible otherwise.

One of the most intriguing aspects of professional sports is superstitions. Intriguing because so many great athletes who have spent years and years training and learning their sports, who go to incredible lengths to prepare for big matches, who know for sure that they are the very best practitioner of their sport in the world, behave as if all their considerable talent will suddenly evaporate if they don't eat the exact same meal every night before a big match.

Bjorn Borg wore the same white Fila clothing every year at Wimbledon. It was a departure from his usual cream-colored outfits and when he won in 1976 he decided not to tempt fate. He put the outfits away at home and kept them preserved, only to be brought out for next year's Wimbledon.

Bjorn was also known to insist on the same practice court every day, at exactly the same time. He was meticulous about his practice, believing that match play will follow practice, so his training schedule was strictly held to.

In the late '70s, I observed Jimmy Connors reading in the corner of the locker room of the Spectrum in Philadelphia prior to a singles match. In his hands was a well-worn single sheet of paper that obviously had been folded and refolded many times. Whatever it was, it was very important to him and when he was done he folded it up, slipped it into a small plastic envelope, and tucked it into his sock. And then he wore it onto the court for his match.

Lots of players over the years have been known to avoid stepping on lines as they walked between points. Even more common is the practice of rearranging the strings on one's racket. But some people just get carried away.

McEnroe went through phases in his career when he would only walk at right angles on the court between points—never diagonally—and even on his way to the umpire to contest a call or throw a tantrum.

Vitas Gerulaitis for years would avoid stepping inside the lines of the court during a change of ends. Coming or going, Vitas would take the long way around. It never applied to walking between points, though, only on the changeovers. Many fans suspected that Vitas's obsessive rewrapping of his racket grip at every changeover was something superstitious, but in fact this was necessary because his hands would sweat so profusely that his grips were soaked after even two games.

Most players' superstitions would last only as long as the winning streak that accompanied them. Eating at the same restaurant each night (and ordering the same meal) was so common that it was taken for granted. How unfortunate when the restaurant happened to be McDonald's! It happened to me twice and earned me two titles.

I can't overemphasize the importance of a positive mental attitude when it comes to succeeding on the tour. There are so many talented players in the world that the difference often comes down to what's inside a player's head. We often remarked in the locker room that there were lots of players in the world who were more gifted or naturally talented than we were, but who just didn't have what it takes upstairs.

Some players even took pride in having overcome a lack of natural talent, proving their determination and drive. To have "gotten the most out of your game" was high praise. In fact, Brad Gilbert won a lot of respect (if not affection) for his habit of "winning ugly." That, of course, is the title of his bestselling book. His ability to "get the most out of what he had" led him to a career in coaching after he retired from competitive play. His successes with Andre Agassi and, later, Andy Roddick are a tribute to his professionalism.

It is said that 90 percent of success is "showing up." That's not far off in the tennis world. I had a lot of potential when I first joined the tour as NCAA champion. I even had a fair amount of success until I got caught up in the distraction of life in the fast lane. The problems came when I stopped "showing up." I didn't show up for practice, or for running, or for mental exercises, sometimes even for matches. I was having too much fun staying out late with Gerulaitis, Nastase, and the rest of the party crowd.

The talent was still there, but the results weren't showing it. It eventually got to be frustrating and demoralizing. The more I wasn't winning, the further my ranking dropped. I wasn't the only one, but my case is symptomatic of how distractions can affect an athlete's professionalism. Of course, that's not the way I saw it—I just thought a lot of things weren't going my way. I blamed the travel, blamed my Fila racket, blamed so many things that eventually I actually believed that I just wasn't happy pursuing this pro tennis player world.

My first dose of reality came at the event in Maui in 1978, and it took a friend to feed it to me. I arrived at Richard Peyton's house in Lahaina with every intention of making that tournament my last for a very long time. From the minute I walked in the door I did nothing but complain about how much I hated tennis and hated life on the tour.

Sunday night we talked late into the night as I explained that

I really wanted to quit the tour but couldn't imagine what else I could do that would pay so well. Richard listened patiently and, finally, when I had talked myself out, he spoke. We had only known each other for a couple of years, since we played each other in the first round of that same tournament two years earlier, but we'd stayed close friends. His reaction floored me. He wondered if that was really why I played tennis—to make a living? It seems he had always thought I played because it was my life.

By some fluke of nature, I won the tournament that week, beating John McEnroe and Peter Fleming along the way. More importantly, I'd gained some perspective that really helped me work my way back up the ladder.

Another friend who helped me climb back up the computer rankings was Peter Morton in Los Angeles. Peter owned the Hard Rock Café and Morton's Restaurant in Los Angeles. He was a real professional who was driven to make a mark in the world, and he was well on his way. It was Peter's influence that got me to realize that life on the road was less about the parties and more about the winning. He was the first to point out that if I partied less and practiced more, I might lose a few "friends," but I'd have a chance to realize some dreams. Peter was right on both counts.

By the time I retired, the social life on the tour had changed dramatically from the early years. During the '70s most players traveled alone and built friendships with their fellow competitors. The old Aussies were famous for fighting like hell on the court and then all going out together for a few beers the same night. As the money got bigger and the stakes were higher, a lot of players spent more time with coaches and supporters, isolating themselves from the competition.

By the end of the '80s, most of the top players seemed to travel in self-contained bubbles, complete with coaches, girlfriends, wives, trainers, and sports psychologists. It had become apparent that these changes were helpful to a player who wanted to maintain a competitive edge over the other players. In some cases, players psyched themselves into bitter rivalries, such as the hatred that Connors and McEnroe used to motivate themselves. In most cases, though, it wasn't animosity at all, just Boris Becker deciding to go to dinner with his entourage the night before the finals rather than have a few beers with Stefan Edberg.

The field of sports psychology made huge progress during the '80s. Self-help programs flourished, led by Tony Robbins, who effectively brought the subject to the masses in a way that wasn't mystical. His books and tapes became bestsellers and made him a superstar worldwide. Tony Robbins was hired by major corporations and famous actors and even the President to consult on motivational psychology. He also dabbled in sports, working briefly with Andre Agassi. The techniques that players adopted certainly helped to improve the state of the art for the sport. As players got bigger and stronger and faster, they also learned to master their emotions and achieve peak mental performance. At the same time, in the psychology of sports, at least on the tennis tour, a player's ranking and overall success were at least partly dependent on lifestyle, social habits, and other factors that had nothing to do with how well he played the sport.

13:

LIVING AND DYING
BY THE COMPUTER

I've SAVED THE MOST significant paradigm shift of our era for last. The ATP computer ranking system.

The *London Daily Telegraph* began unofficially ranking male tennis players at the end of the tennis season in 1914. The first number-one ranking was given by Wallis Myers to the "California Comet" Maurice McLoughlin, the original cannonball server. Ranked fifth was another American, Richard Norris Williams, who had defeated McLoughlin at the U.S. Championship that year. Williams was one of the survivors of the *Titanic*. After he was rescued (having spent hours in waist-deep freezing water), doctors on the *Carpathia* wanted to amputate both his legs. Williams refused and was competing again within three months.

Interestingly, the first number-one ranking issued by the *London Daily Telegraph* didn't go to the Wimbledon champion. In 1914 Australian Norman Brookes defeated Anthony Wilding for the Wimbledon title in an incredible upset. Wallis Myers with the *Telegraph* coranked close friends and Davis Cup teammates Brookes and Wilding second. The fourth slot went to Otto Froitzeim of Germany.

For the most part, the first rankings were viewed as an oddity with little importance. No one really paid much attention to them at all. They did, however, serve a useful purpose, especially for such promoters as C. C. Pyle, who, in 1926, began the first professional tennis troupe centered around Suzanne Lenglen and the top-ranked young American, Vincent Richards.

The USLTA promptly stripped Vincent Richards of his ranking. Bill Tilden, Jack Kramer, and Pancho Gonzalez were early pioneers who also sacrificed their rankings in order to compete professionally. Over the course of several decades, national associations led by the USLTA maintained strict amateur policies and declared any professional to be ineligible for ranking.

When Rod Laver, the player the *London Daily Telegraph* ranked number one in 1961 and 1962, completed the Grand Slam in 1962, he promptly turned pro. He became ineligible for ranking, not reappearing until 1968 when the major tournaments were once again opened to professionals.

Rod Laver topped the chart in '68 (followed by Arthur Ashe, Ken Rosewall, Tom Okker, Tony Roche, John Newcombe, Clark Graebner, Dennis Ralston, Cliff Drysdale, and Pancho Gonzalez). Not surprisingly, when Laver completed an astonishing second Grand Slam in 1969, he again came in at number one (numbers two through ten being Tony Roche, John Newcombe, Tom Okker, Ken Rosewall, Arthur Ashe, Cliff Drysdale, Pancho Gonzalez, Andres Gimeno, and Fred Stolle). For the first time, the tennis world viewed rankings that finally included all amateurs and professionals.

The rankings were still subjective, however, and ideas were bandied about as to ways of ensuring that fairness found its way into the final listings. Eligibility aside, rankings were mostly the personal, subjective, albeit educated, choice of a sportswriter.

In 1970 and 1971, Rino Tommasi ranked players on a statistical basis with all matches included in calculating the best win/loss records. Tommasi ranked Ken Rosewall as the world's number-one player both years.

His action became the precursor to what was the most significant development of our era. In 1973 tennis rankings were taken out of the hands of sportswriters and placed in the "hands" of a computer.

On August 23, 1973, the first computer ranks were released, intended to remove all subjectivity from the rankings by designating points for all matches won in sanctioned events and then calculating a points "average" for each player.

The very first computer-ranked top ten, in order, were: Ilie Nastase, Manuel Orantes, Stan Smith, Arthur Ashe, Rod Laver, Ken Rosewall, John Newcombe, Adrianno Panatta, Tom Okker, and Jimmy Connors. The computer's first year-end rankings still held Nastase at the top and Newcombe and Connors had climbed to second and third.

From its inception, the ATP computer ranking system became the standard of judging the performance of male tennis players and was used as the basis for acceptance of entries and seedings for most major international professional tennis tournaments. A computer gave fair and truly objective entry for tournaments for the first time in the sport; no more quid pro quos; no more secretly held draws (with the rumored exception of Panatta and the Italian Open). Wild cards, of course, would continue to be issued by tournament directors and undoubtedly in some cases the practice was abused, but you'd be hard put to find any player who wanted wild cards to be abolished, and you'd be hard put to find any player who at some point in his career wasn't the beneficiary of a wild card. Primarily, it was the computer that determined who was eligible for a tournament, whether a player would be seeded, whether he'd have to play the qualies.

From a player's perspective, the computer ranking system must itself rank as the greatest advancement toward fair competition in the game's century-long history. Finally a universal truth existed: "Play well and win enough and you will be awarded a ranking commensurate with your abilities regardless of any political influences; the one perfect truth: that number arrives every Monday morning . . . pure, objective, apolitical, honest, and unwavering.

I never competed professionally prior to the use of the ATP computer, but eligibility that hinges on political factors did exist in junior tennis in the United States (still does), and it is not a pleasant experience. It is difficult for me to imagine the nightmares that must have been commonplace prior to the rankings we now take for granted. This shift counts as one of the primary factors contributing to my belief that this generation of players tops all others in the game's history. Naturally, though, as you'd expect, it wouldn't be long before small-minded, power-hungry individuals would threaten the integrity of the computer rankings by using them as a lever in their quest for power.

It was 1982, and the war between WCT and the Grand Prix was just heating up. The MIPTC's efforts to dominate the world of pro tennis eventually led to across-the-board denial of sanctions for WCT events and—gasp—no computer points for results earned in those tournaments (TRANSLATION: Incentive for players to support Grand Prix events and boycott WCT altogether).

The case of Vijay Amritraj, whose ATP ranking plunged from 30 something to 300 something, is undoubtedly the most extreme. Citing my own case as an example, in 1982 I played thirty-some-odd tournaments; only thirteen of them counted as far as the MIPTC was concerned. At the beginning of the year, my ranking was slightly higher than where Vijay's began; we were both ranked in the 30s. At year's end, my ATP rank was 71 despite the fact that I had won one tournament and reached the finals of four others with a smattering of quarterfinal and semifinal finishes in between, and despite the fact that I had posted wins over such notables as Guillermo Vilas, Vitas Gerulaitis, Ilie Nastase, Stan Smith, Adrianno Panatta, and Wojtek Fibak over the course of the year. For consideration with the ATP rankings, it was as if none of those things had occurred at all.

At a press conference held during the tournament in Munich on March 13, 1982, Lamar Hunt, ever subtle, announced the hiring of the German firm Nixdorf to create his own computer ranking, which was to be calculated exactly according to the same criteria as the ATP computer rankings. The only difference was that the Nixdorf computer would include results from WCT events, in addition to all Grand Prix events, Davis Cup, World Team Cup, and the Masters. Nixdorf's very first ranking, released during Wimbledon in 1982, placed Lendl as the number-one player in the world.

At year's end on the ATP computer, I was number 71. On the Nixdorf computer, I was eighth. Other rankings weren't as disparate. McEnroe was ranked number one on both. Lendl was number three with ATP and number two with Nixdorf. Vilas was number four with ATP and number four with Nixdorf.

Most visible among the MIPTC supporters was Arthur Ashe. Retired from competitive tennis several years earlier, Ashe repeatedly encouraged journeymen players to support the Grand Prix Tour by boycotting Hunt's WCT Tour. It's no surprise that Arthur Ashe wasn't able to convince any player to boycott the WCT Tour. The prize money was fantastic all the way down the line, from the winner's check of $100,000 to the first-round loser's pay of $5,000. Additionally, qualifying for the WCT Finals carried with it a bonus of $40,000.

It would have been funny, if it weren't so sad. A billboard advertising the WCT event in Delray proclaimed SEE THE WORLD WAR OF TENNIS. The Grand Prix event opposite Delray on the schedule, the United States Pro Indoor at the Spectrum in Philadelphia, had its own slogan: "Linking the World's *Official* Tennis Tournaments."

In early February the ATP representatives to the Pro Council resigned their seats to place the players in a position of neutrality in the Grand Prix–WCT battle. It was an exercise in futility. Of course the players were caught right in the middle. A pattern emerged where players would enter Grand Prix events for computer points, then jump to the WCT circuit to fatten their wallets—playing both ends against the middle.

Vijay Amritraj, Ivan Lendl, and I were probably the players who were the biggest supporters of WCT, but in fairness I have to say that we were treated just fine by the Grand Prix despite that. There was a little bit of saber rattling levied against Ivan. When he withdrew from a World Team Cup match to play the WCT Championship at Forest Hills, the Pro Council threatened suspension and fined him $10,000. Ivan beat Eddie Dibbs in the final at Forest Hills in forty-nine minutes, earning $2,040.82 a minute. Call it a hunch, but somehow I don't think the $10,000 fine bothered him too much.

At the U.S. Open in 1982, Lendl wore a WCT ball cap at all his press conferences; that legendary Lendl humor at work again.

Lendl played in twelve WCT events in 1982. He won all twelve. He played fourteen Grand Prix events and won five. For the year Lendl won more titles (an astounding seventeen); more matches (an astounding 109); and more money (an astounding $1,528,850) than any other player.

In this battle of the pro tennis tours, there were three primary war weapons:

1. denial of sanction, which Hunt countered by creating his own computer ranking system
2. the attempts by Arthur Ashe and others for a player boycott of WCT events, which the money Hunt offered made laughable
3. the mandate for a ten tournament commitment by players which boomeranged badly when it led to a Borg-less Wimbledon—immediately after Wimbledon the Pro Council was forced to institute what in essence was the "Borg Wild Card Rule": Any player who had won the singles title in the past

three years at a Grand Slam tournament would automatically be admitted into that tournament.

The WCT and Grand Prix stared and placed blame. After two years, the warring factions were at your basic Mexican standoff, so they did the only thing they could. They decided to get along again.

The year 1984 began the great compromise, and tennis was as close to normalcy as it was capable of being. There would be one computer, WCT events were once again sanctioned, and McEnroe was slaughtering everyone in his path—except Ivan Lendl—Mac won thirteen out of fifteen tournaments; 82 out of 85 matches—but Lendl made Roland Garros Mac's Waterloo. Still, when the computer spat out its year-end rankings, it was McEnroe, Connors, and Lendl.

In 1985 Lendl made the U.S. Open his own, and along with it, finally, a number-one ranking. Ivan said, matter-of-factly, "If I deserve to be number one, sooner or later it will show up on the computer." Lendl had become number one in the world, a position he would hold for the next five years until the end of tennis's greatest era.

Lendl's comment on the validity of a number-one ranking was heard by few—and regarded by fewer—but its significance should not be overlooked.

Perhaps no single aspect of tennis deserves greater regard than the computer rankings. Of all the issues I have discussed in this book, the one perfect truth is that number that arrives every Monday morning. Pure, objective, apolitical, honest, and unwavering.

Open tennis brought prize money and recognized professional players as integral to the sport, but the system was still subjective. Political turf wars managed to bring some element of justice to the governance of the sport, but power struggles will continue so long as strong-willed men and women exist and there is a prize worth fighting for.

Bigger prizes and more sponsorship dollars are well deserved, but are not solely responsible for more exciting matches. After all, some of the classic matches were played well before any money was on the line.

Only the computer ranking system has had an entirely positive, constant impact on all aspects of the sport. Its value is unquestioned and I hope, for the future integrity of the sport, it is never compromised.

14:

OUR LEGACY

EVERY GENERATION LEAVES a legacy. If ours had merely been that we offered the world a chance to witness Borg, McEnroe, Connors, Lendl, Becker, Vilas, Gerulaitis, and Nastase—names magical enough to conjure images all these long years later—we'd have served our purpose well, and I'd be proud of my small part in the play.

In fact, our generation offered a lot more.

Sports, like industries or even civilizations, experience turning points in their evolution: people and events that shape history and leave the past behind in favor of new paradigms. Our era was such a time for tennis.

With the advent of open tennis in 1968 came inclusion for all players, amateur and professional, in the major events of the year, along with legitimate prize money available for all. Open tennis ended decades of amateur bias. Finally, professionals were welcomed to Wimbledon, Forest Hills, Roland Garros, and Kooyong. Prize money was legitimate and available above the table.

The formation of the ATP brought an organized, businesslike approach to sharing the responsibility of governing the sport. For the first time in history, professional players commanded a voice in the governance of their sport.

Worldwide media in print and television coverage introduced tennis to a dramatically larger audience. When mass media descended upon the tennis world, it focused a spotlight on the top players and turned them overnight into international celebrities, both for their on-court accomplishments and for their off-court escapades.

Prize money, sponsorships, and endorsements, almost nonexistent before, became commonplace and eventually dominant in the direction of the game and its governance, through the emergence of agents and managers such as Donald Dell and Mark McCormack. The dollar amounts involved, not insignificant in my era, are now staggering.

At his first U.S. Open in 1998, seventeen-year-old Taylor Dent earned $22,000 for playing two singles matches and one doubles match. In 1971 his father, Phil Dent, earned approximately the same amount for playing an entire year on the pro circuit. For winning the 2003 U.S. Open, Andy Roddick walked away with a $1 million paycheck.

With the infiltration of "big money" into the sport, power struggles were spawned that greatly impacted the public side of the sport. Sure it was always there, but now there was *a lot* of money at stake and politics, as usual, made for some very strange bedfellows. Dell, McCormack, Hunt, the ATP, the MIPTC, the WCT . . . all the majors and all the major players elevated the fighting to levels never seen before . . . culminating with a generation of players taking control of their own destiny and forming their own tour.

Of course, our generation will always be defined by Connors, McEnroe, Borg, Lendl, and the rest. But it was also made great by dozens of journeymen like myself who got their fifteen minutes of fame on one court or another and who strove always not just to be good but to be better, to make a mark and somehow join that elite group of stars.

And our legacy was formed by more than just the players. It was agents like Mark McCormack, Donald Dell, Bob Kain, Ion Tiriac, and Bill Riordan. It was leaders like Hamilton Jordan, Lamar Hunt, Michael Davies, and Slew Hester. It was tournament directors like Paul Flory, Bob Briner, Charlie Pasarell, Butch Buchholz, Kobi Hermenjadt, and Owen Williams. ATP staffers like Doug Tkachuk and Weller Evans. It was journalists like Rino Tommasi, Russ Adams, Craig Gabriel, Bud Collins, Mike Lupica, Bob Straus, Fred Mulane, and Peter Bodo. It was support and guidance like Warren Bosworth, Bill Stanley, Bob Mooty, Warren Jacques, Dick Gould, Glenn Bassett, Bob McKinley, Lennert Bergelin, and Bob Brett.

We each played our own game like no generation ever imagined it could be played—both on and off the court. We challenged the status quo, pioneered new technology, tossed out old, tired ideas, and replaced them with bold new thinking. We insisted on meritocracy and fairness in a world dominated by political hacks. We entertained the world in a way few ever imagined it could be done with only courts, rackets, and balls.

In our wake, players who follow our lead entertain massive crowds, competing for obscene paychecks, earning sponsorships and endorsements that secure financial futures for their grandkids. They've long since forgotten what it costs to pay for a hotel room. They take for granted almost unlimited opportunities to play in first-class tournaments and exhibitions. They need never give a thought to the fairness of rankings and just governance of their sport.

And they are boring.

Amazingly talented, brilliant athletes who continue to raise the bar and advance the state of the art *on court*. Bigger, faster, stronger, and better trained than any who ever came before. For now—until they are inevitably eclipsed by those who will follow.

If not for Andre Agassi, they would be on a par with synchronized swimming.

Pete Sampras won more Grand Slam titles than any player in

history—twice as many as John McEnroe, yet he escaped almost unnoticed by the outside world. Can you imagine if John McEnroe had won fourteen Grand Slam titles?

In a piece entitled "Welcome to the Dog Days of Tennis," my friend Bill Dwyre, sports editor of the *Los Angeles Times*, penned the following observation in the summer of 2002:

> . . . There's no there there . . . It is currently a sport of baseline bangers, devoid of drama and purged of personality. It is a tour of young, nice-looking athletes who mostly handle their nomadic existence like robots and exude the same kind of charisma. If R2D2 would take up the game, he'd fit right in. Plus, he might be a better interview.

Maybe all the hard work has been done. Maybe the money just makes it too easy to conform. Maybe the risk of losing all that endorsement money makes it impossible to step outside the lines. Maybe it's just that time in history.

Or maybe we're just a tough act to follow.

DEDICATED TO CATHY LONG

By Sonny Long

WHEN THE THREE OF US—Bill Scanlon, my sister Cathy, and myself—began the process of writing this book, we all learned at least one thing. Any project begins with an idea, a thought, an inspiration.

This book is Cathy's inspiration. As a longtime recreational tennis player, she spent many hours battling "the wall" for exercise. She became a Scanlon fan when he won the NCAA singles championship in 1976 and our stepfather inundated her with newspaper clippings about the Texan's feat.

In early 2002, Cathy asked if I would help her write a book. I am sure I rolled my eyes, but I grudgingly agreed. Her initial idea was to write a biography of Scanlon, and I told her the first thing to do was to get in touch with him to get his approval and cooperation. Cathy was extremely shy, and I am sure the thought of calling Bill out of the blue terrified her.

But she did it.

In talking with Bill, they decided instead of a biography, the book should be about the era of tennis in which Bill played. After all, John McEnroe's book was out, and its self-centered approach to the world of tennis made them both uncomfortable.

Cathy sunk her teeth into the project with vigor, and it wasn't long before the book began to take shape. Cathy found time to nominate Bill for induction into the Texas Tennis Hall of Fame, and we all traveled to Fort Worth in February 2003 to attend the induction ceremonies.

We were all thrilled when Peter Miller of PMA Literary and Film Mangement arranged for St. Martin's Press to publish the book, and we finalized the business arrangements in November of 2003.

On the Sunday before Thanksgiving, Cathy died of a heart attack. She was forty-five years old. She had spent the day researching photos for the book on her computer, as she had done every day for months. She took a break, went outside, and hit a few balls against the wall. Returning inside, she felt ill—pains and sweats—so she called her daughter. She placed a wet cloth on her forehead and lay in bed hoping to feel better.

When I got the call, of course, I was shocked and saddened. Eerily, the day before she died, she had sent me an e-mail with some photos saying I WANTED YOU TO HAVE THESE, IN CASE I DROP DEAD OR SOMETHING.

I think she knew something. I know she taught me something . . . inspiration, dedication, determination. Believe in your idea, work hard, and that idea can become a reality.

I miss her. This book is a lasting vigil to her.